Mennonites in Latin America: Historical Sketches

I0156280

by Jaime Prieto

Bethel College
North Newton, Kansas
2008

Co-published with
Pandora Press
Kitchener, Ontario

Library of Congress Cataloging-in-Publication Data
Prieto, Jaime, 1958-
  [Menonitas en América Latina. English]
  Mennonites in Latin America : historical sketches / by Jaime Prieto.
    p. cm. -- (Cornelius H. Wedel historical series ; 15)
  Includes bibliographical references and index.
  ISBN 1-889239-05-4
  1. Mennonites--Latin America--History--20th century. I. Title.

  F1419.M45P7513 2008
  289.7'8--dc22
                                          2008041667

Wedel Series logo by Angela Goering Miller

ISBN-13: 978-1889239057

www.pandorapress.com

Cornelius H. Wedel Historical Series

Series editor: vols. 1-4, David A. Haury
                 vols. 5-16, John D. Thiesen

Contents

Series Preface

The Cornelius H. Wedel Historical Series was initiated by the Mennonite Library and Archives at Bethel College as part of the college centennial celebration in 1987. Cornelius H. Wedel, the first president of Bethel College from the beginning of classes in 1893 until his death in 1910, was an early scholar of Mennonite studies. His four volume survey of Mennonite history, published from 1900 to 1904, helped to rescue Anabaptism and Mennonitism from their marginal and denigrated portrayal in standard works of church history. Wedel saw Anabaptism and Mennonitism as part of a tradition of biblical faithfulness going back to the early church.

Wedel also believed in the cultivation of the intellect in all fields of knowledge. The current college mission statement continues the commitment to intellectual, cultural, and spiritual leadership for the church and society. The Wedel Series furthers these goals by publishing research in Mennonite studies with a special emphasis on works with a connection to Bethel College, such as campus lecture series and projects based on the holdings of the Mennonite Library and Archives.

Of the fourteen volumes published in the series prior to this time, eleven have originated in campus lecture series or symposia, five arose out of library or archival holdings at Bethel College, and two had both ties. One volume has been reprinted since its original publication. Topics in the series have included Mennonite identity, biography and autobiography, Bethel College history, nonviolent interpretations of United States history, Menno Simons, Mennonite literature, theology, and Mennonite history in various locations.

This volume breaks new ground by being published in both English and Spanish. The Menno Simons lecturer for 2005 at Bethel College was Jaime Prieto, professor of theology at Universidad Bíblica Latinoamericana (Latin American Biblical University) in San José, Costa Rica. This was an entirely new experience for the Menno Simons series: the lectures were given in Spanish, with English translation. We received a glimpse into a new level of Mennonite history, which we now are sharing with a wider audience. Jaime Prieto's ability to make personal connections with the college community and with Spanish-speaking students also made this lecture series one that left a lasting impression. Although the print version here cannot embody the dynamic impact of the original lectures, we hope it gives some taste of the experience.

We wish to thank the following persons for help in bringing these lectures to print: John Driver (who did the original translation from Spanish to English), Laverne Rutschman, C. Arnold Snyder, Linda Shelly, Martha Peterka, Julie Hart, and Jordan Penner.

John D. Thiesen
Series Editor

1
The Polygenetic Character of Mennonites in Latin America 1908-2000

In order to understand the wide variety of groups that make up the family of Anabaptist churches in Latin America it is necessary for us to understand their typology.[1] This typology will permit us to understand the reality of Latin American Anabaptism in our own time, by reconstructing that reality theoretically. In the words of the French sociologist Pierre Bourdieu, typological criteria are built upon the supposition that "there are analogies between the data under immediate study and the totality of the data logically possible from which we select the kind that belong to the case in question."[2]

A typology that takes seriously the relationship between the church and society dare not bypass the monumental contribution of the sociologists Ernst Troeltsch[3] and Max Weber,[4] who envisioned Christianity as a struggle between conformism and protest, between spontaneity and institutionalism, as these derived from the dialectic tension between sects and churches.

The theoretical basis for our choice of criteria for this chronological typology also grows out of a careful examination of the contributions of church historians[5] and sociologists of

---

[1] On the heterogeneous origins of the Anabaptists and the Radical Reformation see John H. Yoder, *Textos escogidos de la reforma radical* (Buenos Aires: La Aurora, 1976), and George Williams, *La reforma radical* (México: Fondo de Cultura Económica, 1983).

[2] Pierre Bourdieu, *Zur Soziologie der symbolischen Formen* (Frankfurt: Suhrkamp, 1974), 29. Cited in Heinrich Schafer, *Protestantismo y crisis social en América Central* (San José: DEI, 1992), 85-86.

[3] Ernst Troeltsch, *El Protestantismo y el mundo moderno* (México: Fondo de Cultura Económica, 1951).

[4] Max Weber, *Die protestantische Ethik: Eine Aufsatzsammlung*, Vol. Y (Gütersloh: Gütersloher Verlagshaus Mohn, 1984), 348-357.

[5] For a history of the church in Latin America we must consider the work of Enrique Dussel, since he takes as his point of departure the multicultural reality of Latin America beginning with the cultures that existed on the continent before the colonial period. See Enrique Dussel, ed., *Historia general de la Iglesia en América Latina, Colombia y Venezuela,* Vol. VII, Columbia and Venezuela, CEHILA (Salamanca: Sígueme, 1981). Other church historians

religion[6] in Latin America, but also in applying their contributions to the Anabaptist realities that have emerged in Latin America. We speak of a chronological typology in order to observe the variety of expressions of Anabaptism in their respective settings.

The categories that we have chosen for our typological study are as follows:

1. Anabaptist churches of foreign missionary origin
2. Anabaptist churches of immigrant origin
3. Anabaptist churches of Latin American origin.

Within these principal categories there are sub-categories of other types of churches that can also be included. We will speak of these as we treat each of the main categories.

The following is a list of the criteria we have used to classify these typologies: the origin of the churches, their organizational forms, their social attitudes and practices within their historical contexts, their ways of carrying on their theological reflection. All of these aspects are inherently tied together and finally determine the character and identity of the various Anabaptist groups. We recognize the need for a deeper study of these criteria in order to arrive at a clearer understanding of these typologies, but for the moment these will help us understand Anabaptism in Latin America.

---

who must be considered for understanding Latin American Protestantism are: Hans Jürgen Prien, *La historia del cristianismo en América Latina* (Salamanca, Spain: Sígueme, 1985); Jean-Pierre Bastian, *Historia del protestantismo en América Latina* (México: CUPSA, 1990); Pablo Alberto Deiros, *Historia del Cristianismo en América Latina* (Buenos Aires: Fraternidad Teológica Latinoamericana, 1992).

[6]The Venezuelan Otto Maduro, for example, looks at the religious panorama in Latin America as: a) a product of religious conflicts, b) as a relatively autonomous ground for social conflicts, and c) as an active factor in religious conflicts. See his book *Religión y conflicto social* (México: Centro de estudios ecuménicos y Centro de reflexión teológica, 1980).

Anabaptist Churches of Foreign Missionary Origin

The principal characteristics of the Anabaptist churches that emerged out of foreign mission initiatives are as follows:[7]

1. Historically, they arose out of missionary initiatives that originated in Anabaptist mission boards in the United States or Canada in order to carry out the foreign missionary efforts of the churches in those countries, or out of the initiatives of missionary agencies formed by the immigrant churches that had already established themselves in the country where the missionary initiative was to be carried out. These churches were characterized by the public preaching of the Word in order to form into congregations those local individuals who responded to their message. Their missionaries were initially supported by the offerings of Mennonite congregations in the United States or Canada, or through the agencies established by the immigrant churches of German origin that had established themselves in Latin America.

2. These Anabaptist churches are made up of nationals but their religious culture, in terms of hymnology, liturgy and congregational organization are of foreign origin – from the United States, Canada, or Germany.

3. The message took on social and charitable dimensions accompanied by the development of a rigid internal ethic rooted in the pietism of the mother churches. To a certain extent this puritanical ethic served as a social defense for these minority groups, in contrast to the somewhat liberal customs found in some immigrant churches that lived together in closed colonies and therefore did not need a strict ethic to protect their culture.

4. The missionary work of these churches was carried out among the lower and middle social classes and among the

---

[7]This characterization is an adaptation of the one proposed by Villalpando for understanding churches of missionary origin. See Waldo Luis Villalpando, "Crisis de las iglesias de inmigración: una hipótesis de trabajo," in: Waldo L. Villalpando (Ed.), *Las iglesias del transplante. Protestantismo de inmigración en la Argentina* (Argentina: Centro de Estudios Cristianos, 1970), 15.

indigenous peoples. In spite of inheriting extraneous organizational and liturgical traditions, worship in these churches was carried out in their own languages of origin. On the other hand, their preaching and their liturgical forms, strongly influenced by foreign missionary patterns, underwent continual processes of adaptation to their national cultural environment.

Churches established by foreign missionary initiative

The first stage (1908-1945)

The Mennonite mission boards in the United States and Canada, as well as those of other historic Protestant denominations such as the Baptists, Methodists, or Presbyterians, began their missionary witness in India, Africa, and Asia toward the end of the nineteenth century.[8] The work of the Mennonite missionary agencies of the United States and Canada in Latin America began at a time when they were beginning to look again toward this "forgotten continent," and especially after the majority of European missionary societies, in their Missionary Conference at Edinburgh (1910), ceased to consider Latin America as a mission field.

We can date the beginning of the work of the North American (U.S. and Canada) Mennonite mission boards in Latin

---

[8]Missionary work in India began thanks to the initiative of the Mennonite Brethren in Russia, of the Mennonite Church, and the General Conference Mennonite Church in the United States. See: Pyarelal J. Malagar, "India," in *Mennonite Encyclopedia,* vol. 5 (Scottdale, Pa.: Herald Press, 1990), 422-427; John Lapp, *The Mennonite Church in India, 1897-1962* (Scottdale, Pa.: Herald Press, 1972).

In 1890 the Mennonite Brethren in Christ began missionary work in Liberia; in 1896 the Defenseless Mennonites sent missionaries to Zaire; in 1898 missionaries from the Brethren in Christ were sent to Zimbabwe. See: James E. Bertsche, "Africa", in *Mennonite Encyclopedia* 5:6-8.

The first missionaries of Dutch origin who arrived in Java from Holland were Pieter Jansz and his wife in 1851. In spite of great difficulty in the face of Moslem hostility, their work was consolidated with the help of Mennonites from Holland, Germany, Switzerland, and Russia. See: Lawrence M. Yoder, "Indonesia," in *Mennonite Encyclopedia* 5:436-438.

America from the time of the First World War. The first Anabaptist churches to emerge in Latin America were the product of the initiative of the Mennonite Board of Missions and Charities of Elkhart, Indiana. As early as 1908 this mission board was being challenged to begin work in Latin America. But it was not until 1911 that they decided to send J. W. Shank to undertake an exploratory trip to Bolivia, Uruguay, and Argentina. Plans were set back by the First World War and it was not until September of 1917 that the Board sent J. W. and Emma Shank and T. K. and Mae Hershey as missionaries to Argentina. In April of 1919 they were able to hold their first public worship service in the city of Pehuajó, location of the first Anabaptist congregation in Latin America.[9]

Missionaries in Argentina in 1919. Adults, left to right: Tobias K. Hershey, Albano Luayza, Mae (Hertzler) Hershey, ?, ?, Emma (Hershey) Shank, Josephus W. Shank, ?. Children, left to right: Lester Hershey?, Beatrice Hershey?, Robert Shank?, Elsie Shank? (The unidentified adults include Francisco Penzotti, secretary for the American Bible Society; and a Schmidt and son, visitors from the United States. (Mennonite Church USA Archives, Goshen, Indiana, Josephus W. Shank papers, Hist. Mss. 1-142, box 1)

The missionaries saw themselves as leaders in a struggle against Roman Catholicism and conservative political parties in their effort to christianize the Latin American peoples and thereby to contribute to the civilizing process in the region. The missionaries saw the Roman Catholic Church, because of its

---

[9] See Lewis S. Weber, *Argentina from Within* (Scottdale, Pa.: Mennonite Publishing House, 1945), 95-96.

collaboration in the colonization of Latin America, as the instigator of inquisitorial methods, characterized by extreme religious intolerance, and as introducing religious practices aimed at achieving the submission of the people, as well as entering into an alliance with the state in order to exercise a monarchical control over the education of the masses.[10] On the other hand, it was commonly held that the Catholic Church had really not evangelized the indigenous peoples, nor had they been helped to emerge from their condition of economic poverty. This was essentially the assessment of missionary J. W. Shank, referring to the mission in Latin America,

> When once we know of the existence of a neighboring continent where millions of Indians live in ignorance and paganism and where many more millions of mixed races have lived for centuries in idolatrous superstition under the name of religion, then our hearts go out in sympathy to them in their need.[11]

Institutions established

The philosophical and theological understandings of the mission boards are also reflected in the ways in which they organized their missionary work in Latin America. First, they were highly interested in the evangelization of people and the formation of congregations. In the educational field they were interested in establishing kindergartens, Bible schools, and printing presses. Their social concerns led them to establish orphanages, medical clinics, and homes for the elderly.[12]

The Mennonite Board of Missions and Charities, after establishing the first Mennonite church in Latin America in Pehuajó, founded a kindergarten. It was hoped that this

---

[10]J. W. Shank, *The Gospel Under the Southern Cross* (Scottdale, Pa.: Mennonite Publishing House, 1943), 26-27.

[11]Ibid., 2.

[12]See Nelson Litwiller, "Our Institutions and their Programs," in J. W. Shank, *Gospel under the Southern Cross,* 130-154.

kindergarten would serve the needs of the surrounding congregations in Pehuajó, Trenque Lauquen, Santa Rosa, Carlos Casares, Tres Lomas and América. During its peak years between 1930 and 1934, there were approximately 344 children enrolled in this kindergarten. The kindergartens also made an important contribution to the evangelization of wider circles in their society since this permitted Mennonite church leaders direct contacts with the parents of the children.

Beginning in 1924, steps were taken to begin a Bible school for the formation of Argentine pastors for ministry in the churches. Trenque Lauquen, and later Pehuajó, became sites for this endeavor and in 1929 the Bible school, under the leadership of missionary J. W. Shank, celebrated its first graduation.

With a view to caring for abandoned children in their midst, an orphanage was opened in 1926. The following year it was moved to Trenque Lauquen under the supervision of missionary Nelson Litwiller. Although the orphanage has long since been closed, the compassion that inspired this vision continues in Pehuajó. Every Sunday poor children are served breakfast before they participate in Sunday school and then are given their noon lunch before returning to their homes, with the local congregation covering all costs.

Serving through the printed page has been another characteristic of Argentine Mennonites. With their printing press they published *El Camino Verdadero*, provided a wide variety of evangelical literature and shared Anabaptist thought in Latin America through the first official publication of the Argentine Mennonite Church, *La Voz Menonita*, beginning in 1932.

In Pehuajó, a nursing home was opened to care for the most needy in the area. As well as offering medical care at their central location, nurses frequently made house calls to care for patients. Another social service initiative was the creation of a home for the elderly that was begun, thanks to the donation of

La Voz Menonita

SUMARIO

Pág.

EDITORIAL .... A. Lenyza   1
¿Quiénes son los Menonitas? .... N. Litwiler   2
La Obra Misionera de los Menonitas T. K. Hershey 4
La Otra Menonita en la Argentina A. Lenyza   7
La Argentina como Campo Misionero S. Battaglia 11

DOCTRINAS BIBLICAS

No-Resistencia .... T. K. Hershey Jr.
La Santificación .... F. Cavadore 15
La Adoración .... J. L. Butt   17
La Abnegación .... W. G. Lauver 19

Organo de la Iglesia Menonita en la República Argentina

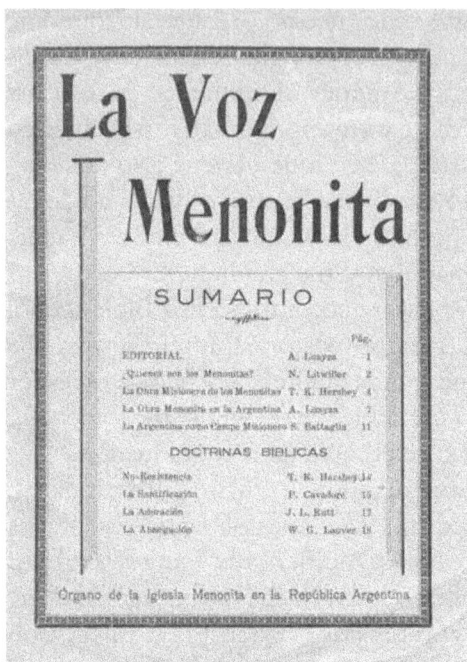

First issue of La Voz Menonita, *March 1932.*
(Mennonite Church USA Archives, Bethel College, North Newton, Kansas)

the land on which the buildings were eventually built, by Mr. and Mrs. Besoytaorube, the first couple to become members of the congregation.

Internal organization

The mission boards generally reproduced their own organizational patterns in the national churches that emerged in Latin America. After churches were established in Argentina, a bishop was named to oversee all the congregations. By the 1940s, all the regions where congregations had been established were divided into two principal zones. The eastern zone had the following districts: a) Bragado with seven churches; b) Carlos Casares with seven churches and c) Pehuajó with four congregations. The western zone was also divided into three districts: a) Trenque Lauquen with six congregations; b) América with four churches and c) Cosquín with three congregations. A bishop was charged with overseeing each zone and a superintendent was assigned to each district.

Within the organizational scheme there was also a Mission Council, made up of missionaries, from the time that the work had been begun in Argentina. It was this Council that initiated official contacts with the mission board in North America. On the other hand, beginning in 1923, annual conferences were held with representation from all of the Argentine Mennonite churches. From this assembly an Argentine board was formed, made up of the missionaries together with some of the Argentine church leaders. This kind of organization was typical of the Mennonite churches in Latin America that had been founded under the auspices of foreign mission boards. This led to marked dependence on the pastoral leadership of the missionaries and also to a notable degree of economic dependence. Overcoming this stage of dependence in both personnel and economic affairs was not easy for the Mennonite organizations. Even today, after so many years of mission activity, one notes a marked degree of dependence on the mission boards in the United States and Canada in many Latin American churches.[13]

The second historical stage of the Anabaptist churches initiated by foreign mission boards (1945-1989)

We set our second historical stage of the missionary enterprise in Latin America undertaken by mission boards in the United States and Canada in the period following the Second World War. During this new era, North American hegemony in politics, economics, culture, and religion was felt throughout the Latin American continent. The explosion of Mennonite missionary activity in Latin America must be seen in the context of the development model that gained prominence during the Cold War. This will be apparent, especially when we analyze carefully the social message missionaries communicated in the context marked by the Cuban Revolution in the decade of the 1960s and later by the revolutionary movements in Central America during the decades of the 1970s and 1980s.

It is interesting to note how the earliest mission efforts of the immigrant Mennonite churches among their indigenous neighbors were characterized from their very beginnings by the same missionary strategies as those generally used by foreign missionary agencies in founding churches. Even among the mission boards representing smaller Anabaptist groups in the United States and Canada we note a marked interest in evangelizing among the Spanish-speaking mestizo population as well as among indigenous peoples, in their own native

---

[13]T. K. Hershey, "Problems of Organization and Finance," in J. W. Shank, *Gospel under the Southern Cross,* 155-166.

languages. Since these two types of missionary witness each have their own particular character, we will refer to them briefly. We will use, as examples, the work of the Conservative Mennonite Conference of Ohio (CMC) in Costa Rica and that of the Washington-Franklin County Mission Board-Eastern Mennonite Board of Missions and Charities (EMBMCH) in Guatemala.

Spanish-speaking Anabaptist churches

The beginnings of the mission enterprises of both the CMC in Costa Rica as well as the EMBMCH in Guatemala are tied to the exploratory trips of Orie Miller.[14] Miller served as Executive Secretary of Mennonite Central Committee from 1920 to 1958 and as Associate Secretary of EMBMCH. Miller understood very well the political, social, and religious situation in Latin America. He not only initiated contacts with governments, making possible the migration of Mennonite refugees from Europe to Anabaptist colonies in Latin America, but also greatly facilitated the work of Anabaptist mission boards in Latin America. It was following his investigation trip to Central America, accompanied by Raymond Schlabach of CMC in June of 1961,[15] that this mission board decided to initiate mission work among the Hispanic population in the central valley of Costa Rica. The same thing happened in Guatemala. During a trip in June of 1966, Orie Miller, accompanied by Earl Grof and James Hess, missionaries serving under the auspices of EMBMCH,[16] decided to begin mission work among Hispanics in Guatemala City.

---

[14]Paul Erb, *Orie O. Miller, The Story of a Man and an Era* (Scottdale, Pa.: Herald Press, 1969).

[15]Orie Miller, Raymond Schlabach, "Findings-Suggestions-Recommendations," Orie Miller and Raymond Schlabach to Conservative Mennonite Mission Board, Deputation Assignment to Central America, June 8-16, 1960, (ACMCUSA).

[16]Francisco Bernal González, *Historia de la Iglesia Menonita en Guatemala,* Primera promoción (Guatemala: Tesina del Instituto Bíblico Menonita de Guatemala, 1984), 1.

It is interesting to note that the evangelistic work of both mission boards always included a social dimension. From the very beginning, there was an effort to combine evangelization and the formation of churches with the active participation of young North American voluntary service workers in community development and agricultural work in rural areas. However the creation of social institutions such as medical dispensaries, orphanages, printing presses, and homes for the elderly would no longer be given the same priority it had in an earlier period, as had been the case of the Mennonite Church in Argentina.

During the early stages of its development, the leadership of the Costa Rican Mennonite Church was in the hands of missionaries. At the beginning, Elmer and Eileen Lehman and Henry and Esther Helmuth, together with young North American voluntary service personnel, gave leadership to this missionary witness. It was not until the mid 1970s that the Costa Ricans began to share more directly in the church's leadership. Coming from a mission board which was still heir to certain Amish customs,[17] the earliest CMC missionaries stood out for the way they dressed, men with dark suits and clerical collars and their wives with long skirts and their characteristic prayer coverings. It proved to be impossible to sustain these practices for long. Their new Costa Rican members saw that other Protestant churches did not require a prayer veiling. And to reject the practice still in vogue among the older women in the Catholic churches, they decided that they would no longer wear their veils in church. There was considerable disagreement on matters of dress during the early years, but the missionaries finally ended up adapting to the dress practices of the members of Costa Rican Protestant churches.

On the other hand, missionaries from U. S. and Canadian mission boards proved to be very respectful toward Costa Rican Protestantism. The percentage of Protestants compared to Roman Catholics was very low. Therefore it was necessary to form alliances with other sectors of Protestantism in Costa Rica. For example, early in its liturgical life, the emerging church

---

[17]See Ivan J. Miller, *History of the Conservative Mennonite Conference 1910-1985* (Grantsville, Md.: Ivan J. and Della Miller, 1985), 28-70.

chose *Himnos de la Vida Cristiana*[18] as their hymnal. This was the hymnal already used by the majority of Baptist and Protestant churches in the country. When a new Mennonite hymnal was introduced in the early 1970s it would be more along the line of the charismatic movement that was profoundly influencing the life of Central American Protestantism.

The dominant ideology of the Mennonite missionaries who went to Costa Rica in respect to the relation of church and society was not very different from that of those who were sent by other North American missionary agencies. They held that there should be a clear separation of church and state. But they also thought that the development programs carried out by local governments and those like "Alliance for Progress," sponsored by the United States, were practical solutions to the socio-political problems of Central America. On the other hand, their mission programs were oriented more toward the poor and middle classes. Even though the missionaries exercised a considerable ideological influence upon national church leaders, we should recognize that some sectors of the Anabaptist churches assumed notably critical attitudes toward prevailing injustices and the militaristic and interventionist policies of the United States during the revolutionary period in Central America.[19] In the case of the Mennonites in Honduras there were national church leaders who assumed a pastoral practice and undertook theological reflection oriented by a Latin American theology of liberation. They worked together with other institutions such as Mennonite Central Committee in processes of mediation and peacemaking in times of war. Other Mennonites in Honduras, in contrast, assumed somewhat conservative charismatic pastoral practices that left unchallenged the political, economic, and military problems that plagued the region.[20]

---

[18]*Himnos de la Vida Cristiana: Una colección de antiguos y nuevos Himnos de Alabanza a Dios* (Nueva York: Alianza Cristiana y Misionera, 1967).

[19]See James Adrián Prieto V., *Die mennonitische Mission in Costa Rica (1960-1978)* (Hamburg: Verlag an der Lottbek, 1992), 93-207.

[20]Jorge Rodríguez, "Evolución de la Iglesia Evangélica Menonita Hondureña" (Thesis, Seminario Bíblico Latinoamericano, 1994).

Anabaptist churches that retain their indigenous language

CMC's interest in carrying out mission among indigenous peoples is well expressed in the following missionary imperative. "The world needs the Gospel in: a) Translation because there are yet 2,000 tribes, or 1,000 languages and dialects who haven't any part of the Gospel in their language. b) Proclamation because it is God's plan to save others through the instrumentality of those who are saved. c) Demonstration because creeds and sermons are worn threadbare, and a world in need looks for Christianity that contains genuine reality."[21]

At the same time that the mission to Spanish-speaking people in Costa Rica was being initiated, missionary work began among the indigenous peoples in the valley of Talamanca in their native language, Bri-Bri. R. Schlabach was the missionary who began this witness in 1961 among the Bri-bries and dedicated himself to translating the Bible into their language.[22] The same can be said for the EMBMCH in Guatemala, where missionary witness among the Spanish-speaking population and the indigenous peoples were initiated simultaneously. While Lois and Richard Landis began mission work among Hispanics in Guatemala City, the Lehmans dedicated themselves to a study of Kekchi in order to work in Alta Verapaz.

The missionary witness undertaken by CMC among the indigenous peoples in Costa Rica developed differently from that of the EMBMCH in Guatemala. The churches in the area of Talamanca were always related to the Conference of Evangelical Churches of Costa Rica (CIEMCR). Even though many of their songs and their Bible readings are in their own Bri-Bri language, they have never wanted to separate themselves from their sister Spanish-speaking Mennonite congregations who belong to CIEMCR. This is probably because the number of Bri-Bri speakers in Costa Rica is very small.

---

[21]Jesse Zook, "The Missionary Imperative," *Missionary Bulletin* 7:9 (Sept. 1958): 6.

[22]Jaime Adrián Prieto V., *Indianermission im Tal von Talamanca, Costa Rica (1891-1987)* (Hamburg: Verlag an der Lottbek, 1995), 199.

In Guatemala the situation has been different. In spite of the fact that the missionary work among Hispanics and among the indigenous Kekchi were initiated simultaneously by workers under the auspices of the same mission board, almost from the very beginning there were notable differences between the Spanish-speaking and the indigenous churches.[23] The tension began in the "New Jerusalem" Mennonite Church, growing initially out of the missionary work of the Lehmans in Alta Verapaz. The first national pastor of this congregation in the early 1970s was an indigenous brother, Pablo Tzul. Later other pastors of Hispanic origin from Guatemala City collaborated in pastoral roles. It was to be expected that internal contradictions would present themselves in a church attended by both Spanish speakers and others of the Kekchi tradition. There were some discussions about charismatic-pentecostal influences that some of the Hispanics brought with them. However, the same social and ethnic conflicts that Guatemalan society embodies boiled over into the internal life of the congregation. The North American missionaries understood the seriousness of the conflict between Hispanics and the indigenous Kekchi and therefore favored a solution that would encourage the development of an indigenous Kekchi church. The Kekchi-speaking Guatemalan National Evangelical Mennonite Church thus developed as an organization independent from the Conference of Evangelical Mennonite Churches of Guatemala, which is the organization that includes the Spanish-speaking congregations.

The influence of the mission board is noticeable in the internal organization of the Kekchi Mennonite churches in Guatemala. There is a board of directors, a pastors' meeting, an annual assembly of the Conference, regional councils, and a series of national organizations such as a Finance Committee, an Evangelization Committee, a Social Service Committee, and a Bible Institute. Minutes are kept of all the meetings of the Board of Directors in Kekchi and of the annual conferences in

---

[23]A recorded interview made by Jaime Prieto with Francisco Bernal, ex-pastor of the "New Jerusalem" Mennonite Church in San Pedro Carchá, Guatemala, Wednesday, March 19, 1996.

Spanish.[24] These organizational structures reflect the models brought to them by representatives of the North American mission boards. But they also reflect the requirements of the Guatemalan government, which offers legal status to religious associations and requires that the minutes of their general assemblies be kept in Spanish thereby achieving its purpose of ordering and controlling all civic and indigenous organizations.

Anabaptist churches established by immigrant congregations in Latin America (1935-1945)

It should be noted in this typology that missionary activity among indigenous peoples as well as among Spanish-speaking populations has also been carried out by the German immigrant churches of European origin that were established in Latin America. Due to limitations of time we will take the churches of Paraguay as an example, but we will refer only to their work among indigenous peoples.

Indigenous language Anabaptist churches

Historical background of the immigrant churches

Among the Anabaptist immigrants who arrived in Latin America were those so involved in their struggle for survival that they did not participate overtly in missionary activity. They will be mentioned later. But we also have stories of immigrant congregations which became involved in missionary work among the Hispanic and indigenous populations in Latin America. An example of these are the German-speaking immigrant Mennonites who settled in Paraguay and founded the colonies of Menno (1926), Fernheim (1929) and Neuland (1941-1943) in the Chaco.

---

[24]See Roberto Caal, "Libro de Actas de la Secretaría de la Asamblea General de la Iglesia Nacional Evangélica Menonita Guatemalteca," Municipio de San Pedro Carchá, Alta Verapaz, Guatemala, September 6, 1982, 10-15. (AINEMG).

Menno Colony was founded by immigrants from the Old Colony and Sommerfelder Mennonites living in Manitoba, Canada. They decided to migrate because of the new laws being passed by the Canadian government that, beginning at the time of the First World War in 1914, prohibited the use of the German language and the teaching of religion in state and private schools. Fernheim Colony was established in 1930 with the arrival of 2,001 German-speaking immigrants from the Soviet Union. And Neuland Colony was founded by German-speaking Mennonite immigrants fleeing from Russian territories after the invasion of the Soviet Union by German armies between 1941 and 1945.[25]

It could be said that the mission work initiated by these immigrant congregations, like those in the colonies just mentioned, had its roots in their desire to share the Gospel with indigenous peoples. But it also became a necessity, since the lands granted by the Paraguayan government to the German-speaking immigrants had originally been occupied by these indigenous peoples. Since these peoples continued living in the vicinity, the immigrants thought it imperative that they become "civilized," receiving an education that would equip them to become self-sufficient.

This initiative was taken in Fernheim Colony in 1935 when, following the Chaco War, a mission board known as "Licht den Indianern" was formed. The board was established for the following purposes: evangelization, education, health, and economic assistance. The indigenous people known as the "Enlhet" (Lengua) was the first recipient of this missionary activity.

The nature of the immigrants' work with the indigenous people

The church begun by the immigrants grew out of a desire to evangelize and civilize the indigenous community. Therefore an evangelistic program was developed which called for the

---

[25]Hans J. Wiens, *Dass die Heiden Miterben seien: Die Geschichte der Indianersmission im paraguayischen Chaco* (Paraguay: Konferenz der Mennonite Brudergemeinden in Paraguay, 1989), 25-27.

translation of the Bible into the languages of the people – Enlhet (Lengua) and Nivaclé (Chulupí). Missionary Dietrich Lepp was in charge of the translation of the Bible into the Enlhet language and Gerhard Hein worked on the Nivaclé translation. The missionaries used films in their evangelization of the Chulupies. In the case of the Enlhet, preaching was done with the help of a Lengua preacher who had come to them from an English mission called "La Promesa" (The Promise). In the indigenous reservations at Yalve Sanga and Campo Largo (both these communities bordered on Mennonite colonies) it was essential to organize Bible schools for the training of the new indigenous believers.

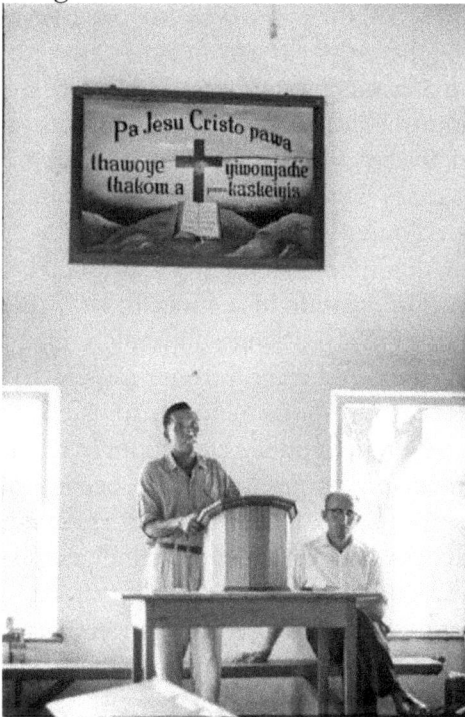

Chulupí church in Filadelfia, Paraguay, ca. 1964.
(Mennonite Church USA Archives, Bethel College, North Newton, Kansas. Photographer Nancy Flowers, Standard Oil Company.)

The development programs among the indigenous were important for the German-speaking immigrants, because they wanted them to achieve their economic independence and thereby not need to depend upon the immigrant colonies for their subsistence. This led the Mennonite immigrants to share their agricultural expertise thereby changing their indigenous neighbors from a semi-nomadic lifestyle to a sedentary one supported by their own agricultural production. It should be noted that in this process it was the indigenous workers who performed the physical labor and the Mennonite colonies who organized the economic structures. In this way indigenous colonies were organized, with the help of

Mennonite Central Committee in 1960, to acquire the necessary lands.

Another aspect of indigenous life which was profoundly influenced by the immigrant Mennonites was the notably communitarian way of life which characterized the latter. They had developed a system of production and economic organization based on cooperatives. The Mennonites tried to help their indigenous neighbors organize and operate their own cooperatives, although they continued to oversee the granting of credits as well as their economic operations.

In the health programs that the immigrants organized for their indigenous neighbors and in the introduction of modern medicines for the treatment of their ills, we also observe a certain paternalism. During the early years (from 1954), a health station under the direction of a nursing staff was established. By 1968 there was a full time medical doctor in charge with a capacity of 59 beds and 9 clinics under the supervision of nurses. The most urgent cases were referred to the hospitals located in the Mennonite colonies.

Another dimension of this missionary activity among the Chulupies and Lenguas was the creation of schools. In 1937 the first school was opened in Yalve Sanga in which eight indigenous students received their education from a missionary teacher. Later in 1961 part of this responsibility was transferred to the state as a part of its program of public education. In all of this process it is interesting to note that what began as instruction from German-speaking teachers was later assumed by Spanish-speaking teachers and eventually by indigenous teachers using their own languages.

Groups within the German immigrant congregations, such as women's organizations and youth groups, all contributed to the formation of these new indigenous congregations. These groups participated in the tasks of evangelization (Bible teaching) and manual arts (cooking and sewing) for Chulupi and Lengua women in order to help them become more self-sufficient. The impact of the immigrant colonies on the lifestyles of the indigenous young people led to notable cultural changes. For example, the custom among the indigenous youths of marrying at a very young age changed notably as new cultural paradigms were introduced by the immigrants.

Criticisms and challenges arising out of immigrant interaction with indigenous people (Enlhet)

This meeting of peoples, so diverse in terms of their ethnicity, culture, and language has not been easy. The Paraguayan anthropologist Miguel Chase-Sardi, the German anthropologist Walter Regehr, the sociologist Calvin Redekop, and the church historian Titus Guenther have all given us different versions of the tensions and the complexities of the situation produced by two very diverse peoples living together in close proximity.[26] Once the occasions for greatest tension between the interests of the indigenous communities and the progress of German-speaking immigrants were at least partially resolved, we note the resurgence of the Enlhet communities. The indigenous communities have received the Gospel that came to them through the evangelistic efforts of the immigrant missionaries and have organized their ecclesial community under the name "Convención de los Hermanos Evangélicos Enlhet de Ya'alvc-Saanga." At the same time, their own identity has been reaffirmed through an effort to record in their own language their oral traditions, their cultural customs, their botanical knowledge and their own spirituality which is closely tied to the lands of the Gran Chaco.[27] Without doubt the

---

[26]Miguel Chase-Sardi, *La situación actual de los Indígenas en el Paraguay* (Asunción: Centro de estudios antropológicos, Universidad Católica, 1972); Walter Regehr, *Die lebensräumliche Situation der Indianer im paraguayishen Chaco. Humangeographische-ethnologische Studie zu Subsistenzgrundlage und Siedlungsform akkulturierter Chacovölker* (Basel: Geographische-Ethnologischen Gesellschasft Basel, 1979); Calvin Redekop *Strangers Become Neighbors: Mennonite and Indian Relations in the Paraguayan Chaco* (Scottdale, Pa.: Herald Press, 1980); Titus Guenther F., "Cambio social sin violencia: La convivencia indígena-menonita del Chaco paraguayo," in *Comunidad Teológica de Chile, Revista Teología en Comunidad. Cultura e Historia,* Julio 1991, 25-41.

[27]See the bibliography of the enormous dictionary written in this community in its language Enlhet: Ernesto Unruh and Hannes Kalisch, *Moya'ansaeclha'Nengelpayvaam Nengeltomha Ehlhet* (Yal"alve-Saanga: Comunidad Enlhet). See Ernesto Unruh and Hannes Kalisch, "Defender nuestro

immigrant colonies face great challenges: how to be more faithful to their Kingdom calling in just and fraternal relationships with their neighbors, the Enlhet. For the Enlhet, their challenge is to be able to accept the present social reality, and at the same time to reaffirm contextually the enormous riches of their own culture. The Mennonite congregations of indigenous origin can contribute much in terms of culture, spirituality, and wisdom to the Mennonites in Latin America.

Anabaptist churches of immigrant origin (1921-2000)

By Anabaptist churches of immigrant origin we mean a definite ethnic-religious group made up of immigrants and descendants of immigrants of principally German origin that does not practice conversion. Other characteristics are: a) they originally use the language of the country from which they have emigrated, b) originally they are considered part of the church of the country from which they have emigrated (theme of nationalization).[28]

The Anabaptist churches of immigrant origin that arrived in Latin America, fleeing from the World Wars that broke out in Europe, can be classified in two groupings according to the characteristics mentioned earlier: a) the ethnic church of immigrants and b) the ethnic church of naturalized immigrants.

The ethnic Anabaptist church of immigrants

The earliest ethnic Anabaptist churches of immigrants in Latin America were made up of the waves of Mennonite immigrants known as the "Altkolonier" (Old Colony). These

---

idioma," *Revista Acción* 30 (March 1988): 34-36. Hannes Kalisch, "Moya'ansaeclha'Nengelpayvaam Negeltomha Enlhet," *Mennoblatt* 68:20 (October 16, 1997): 8-10.

[28]Definition based on Christian Lalive d'Espinay, "Acomodación o reforma? Hacia una sociología de las iglesias de inmigración en la Argentina," in Waldo Luis Villalpando (Ed.), *Las iglesias del trasplante* (Argentina: Centro de Estudios Cristianos, 1970), 162.

groups from their very beginnings were related to Anabaptist groups which had originated in the Low Countries like Holland, Belgium and Friesland. They spoke "Plattdeutsch" daily, but in their churches and schools they used High German. Around the end of the eighteenth century, by invitation of the Czarist government of Russia, thousands of them migrated to Ukraine. There, in 1788-89, they formed the Chortitza Colony on the shores of the Dnieper River, and the Molotschna Colony. Later, in 1874-1880 some 7,000 Mennonites from these colonies emigrated to Canada. The original guarantees they had received regarding their freedom to develop their own religious schools were compromised when, in 1917, the provincial government of Manitoba decided that the Mennonite colonies must adapt to the requirements of the provincial educational system, including the use of the English language. For this reason these colonies decided to migrate to another country where their wishes to educate their children in their own language and culture would be respected. In 1921 the president of Mexico, General Alvaro Obregón, authorized the sale of lands to facilitate colonization of San Antonio de los Arenales, thereby leading to a new wave of migration. Approximately 6,000 members of the Canadian Mennonite colonies moved to Mexico.[29]

Among these groups we find Mennonites from the Soviet Union, in a contingent of approximately 1,200 persons, who in 1929 had spent a year in Germany. The following year they emigrated to southern Brazil where they settled in the state of Santa Catarina. These Anabaptists entered Brazil as refugees under the auspices of the German Red Cross with the help of the Hanseatic Colonization Society. The area assigned to them for colonization was called Krauel and consisted of three villages: Witmarsum, Gnadenthal, and Waldheim.[30] The

---

[29]See Walter Schmiedehaus, *Die Altkolonier-Mennoniten in Mexiko* (Winnipeg, Manitoba: Mennonitische Post, 1982).

[30]On the early experiences of Mennonite immigrants in Brazil see Peter Pauls, Jr., *Urwaldpioniere, Persönliche Erlebnisse Mennonitischer Siedler aus den ersten Jahren am Krauel und von Stolzplateau, S.C.* (Witmarsum: Festkommission der Jubiläumsfeier, 1980).

Mennonites of Witmarsum speak principally Low German[31] and hold to their traditional ethnic standards. In the case of the Witmarsum Colony, two different congregations were formed: the Mennonite Brethren (Mennoniten Brudergemeinde) and the Mennonite Church (Mennoniten Gemeinde). The Mennonite Brethren had emerged as a result of a division among the Mennonites in the Soviet Union in 1860 when differences arose between Mennonite property owners and their brethren who owned no property. This difference was also reflected in the decision to emigrate to Latin America. A third congregation later formed in Witmarsum called *Igreja Menonita Evangélica Livre* (Freie Evangelische Mennoniten Gemeinde). This group attempted to reconcile the differences between the other two groups as well as integrate German-speaking members who came from other denominational backgrounds.

Another example of ethnic immigrant Anabaptist churches is found in Uruguay. Mennonite emigrants from Prussia and Poland settled in Uruguay in 1948, establishing the colonies of El Ombu, Gartenthal, Delta and Nicolich.[32] These German-speaking Mennonite families became refugees when the Russian army occupied sections of West Prussia in the area of the Vistula and Nogat Rivers, forcing them to flee for their safety.

Organization

A prominent characteristic of the congregational organization among these ethnic immigrant Anabaptists is the important role played by their overseer minister known as *Der Ältester* (Elder). This person assumes the primary responsibility for the life of the congregation and usually guides discussions in the congregational council. Other ministers are known as *Prediger* (Preacher) and charged with helping the Elder in the

---

[31]Herbert Minnich, "Organizaçao religiosa," in *Altiva Pilatti Balhana y Brasil Pinheiro Machado, Campos Gerais. Estructuras Agrárias* (Paraná: Universidad Federal do Paraná, Facultade de Filosofía, 1968), 157.

[32]See Johannes Bergmann, *En Uruguay encontramos una nueva patria. Historia de la inmigración de los mennonitas provenientes de Danzig, Prusia y Polonia* (Uruguay: Imprenta Mercur S.A., 1998), 17.

tasks of ministry and preaching. The Elder generally carries responsibility for several congregations and is in charge of presiding over the Lord's Supper, baptisms, and marriages. A deacon is in charge of congregational finances and helps the Elder to serve the communion bread and wine at the Lord's Supper.[33] Normally the Elder is chosen to serve for an indefinite term, while preachers and deacons are elected to definite terms. The congregational council (*Gemeindevorstand*) is made up of the Elder and two officials elected from the congregation. These may either be ordained or lay persons. And finally, there is the general assembly, made up of all of the members of the congregation. Supreme authority lies with this body as they meet in assembly (*Gemeindestunde*) to make important decisions affecting the life of the community. This type of organization is characteristic of all the different groups of Anabaptist immigrants in Latin America. This is true of the Mennonites in the Witmarsum Colony as well as the immigrant Mennonites in Uruguay, who when their elder Leonhard Ratzlaff died during their flight from Poland, met as a group on the *Volendam*, the ship that took the group to Uruguay, and drew up official minutes organizing thereby the congregation of the Mennonites in Uruguay.[34]

Ethnic church of naturalized immigrants (1970-1999)

The ethnic church made up of naturalized immigrants includes the second and third generation descendants of the earliest Mennonite immigrants among whom there is a definite inclination to become naturalized citizens in their host country. These new generations who have resided since birth in their new country relate to their society and develop a natural appreciation for its culture, language, and national identity. It is not uncommon to find an inter-generational tension between the early immigrants with their attachment to the German language and the customs of their origins in Germany and

---

[33]Herbert Minnich, "Organizaçao religiosa," 159.
[34]Johannes Bergmann, *En Uruguay encontramos una nueva patria,* 43-44.

Russia and the new generations, where many of their young people are beginning to marry persons from the host country.

Vila Guaira church in 1985. *(Mennonite Church USA Archives, Bethel College, North Newton, Kansas)*

Vila Guaira in Curitiba, Brazil, provides a clear example of this ethnic church of immigrants. Peter Siemens is the current pastor of this congregation. His parents are Peter and Lisa Klassen Siemens who, when they were very young, emigrated from the Ukraine to Brazil in 1931. Originally they were a part of the Witmarsum Colony. Peter Siemens belongs to the first generation that was born and reared in Brazil. He identified deeply with the missionary efforts of the Mennonites among the Brazilian people and became a pastor in several of their congregations. His wife is Brazilian by birth. But now, Peter and his wife have returned to give pastoral leadership in an ethnic congregation of German-speaking Mennonite immigrants where, together with another pastoral associate, they lead the congregation in worship in both German and Portuguese. The church in Vila Guaira is an example of congregations of German-speaking immigrant origin in the process of transition. They provide space for those of earlier generations who desire to maintain their cultural traditions as well as the new generations whose friendships and mixed marriages also require the use of the Portuguese language.[35]

But we should also take note of the fact that recently the Vila Guaira congregation suffered a painful division when a considerable group of members separated themselves to form another church which they call "The Mennonite Church of the New Covenant." Many factors contributed to this separation but some were related to the process of acculturation that the

---

[35]Information based on a recorded interview of the author with Peter Siemens, pastor of Vila Guaira, ISBIM, Curitiba, Brazil, Tuesday, November 30, 1999.

congregation is going through. The new congregation does not continue to use both languages in its worship services. They are held only in Portuguese. "The Mennonite Church of the New Covenant" is an example of the radical transition process in the church from its old Russo-German roots to its new Brazilian culture.

Organization

In the experiences of these churches we also see major organizational changes taking place. Some vestiges remain of the organizational forms we noted earlier in the ethnic congregations of immigrants where Elders, who were the keepers of the tradition, played an important role. But now we begin to see pastors playing a much larger role. In the new congregations made up of the descendants of immigrants who are becoming incorporated into Brazilian society, we note that the congregational structures are no longer those of the immigrant community. The role of the pastors and the local church structures are becoming much more like those that characterize the congregations initiated by missionary activity. In the case of the Vila Guaira congregation, Peter Siemens commented that his evangelistic interest is, in comparison to the new "Mennonite Church of the New Covenant," much more discreet.

Anabaptist churches of Latin American missionary origin (1919-2000)

We have noted the diversity of the Anabaptist churches established in Latin America. Some grew out of the work of foreign mission boards in the United States and Canada. Others originated out of the missionary witness of German-speaking immigrant churches. It is this reality that explains the diversity of the Latin American churches. We will now note briefly the missionary initiatives of Latin American Anabaptist churches resulting in the emergence of new congregations on the continent. Their typology finds its roots in the early work of the

North American mission boards in Latin America and we began with the early phase of evangelization in Argentina because we consider that from the very beginning the Latin Americans are the ones who are the primary agents of evangelization.

The characteristics of the Anabaptist churches of Latin American missionary origin are as follows:

a) Latin Americans were the principal agents of evangelization in the towns and communities where the missionaries from the United States and Canada established the first Anabaptist congregations.

b) The evangelization and the establishing of churches were shaped by cultural, economic, and social aspects unique to the places where these churches were formed by Latin American families.

c) The historical stages in which Latin Americans assumed all the administrative, teaching, and pastoral responsibilities in these Latin American congregations, as well as the establishing of new congregations, varies from one country to another. It is not the same to speak in that sense of a church with such a long history, like the churches in Argentina that were begun early in the past century, as it is of the Evangelical Mennonite Church in El Salvador that was established in 1979.

d) During the periods of rapid revolutionary changes rooted in Latin American nationalism, the churches that emerged manifested their own organizational dynamics, their own cultural forms and hymnology, and their own ways of reinterpreting Anabaptist church practice and theology.

e) That a mission emerges in Latin America thanks to Latin American missionary initiatives does not necessarily mean that it will be characterized by autonomy or be an authentic expression of local culture. In many cases new Latin American missionary enterprises turn out to be models copied from mission organizations of North American origin and not necessarily in the Mennonite tradition.

f) New forms of mission are arising among Mennonites in Latin America in response to the challenges of burgeoning metropolitan centers.

Mennonite churches in Latin America that grew out of a natural process of evangelization

The emergence of new Mennonite communities and congregations as a result of the evangelization done by families of an established Mennonite congregation, or by Mennonite families that moved from one location to another and then began a new Mennonite congregation is probably the most natural and the most successful way to carry out mission in Latin America.

The first example is precisely what occurred in Argentina during the early period from 1919 to 1933. It is true that we need to recognize the work of the mission board, but we also need to recognize the fact that many of the 21 places of mission witness were opened thanks to the arduous efforts of many Argentine brothers and sisters. We note especially the work of the colporteurs who moved about in their "Bible Wagon" carrying with them the Word and evangelistic tracts to many towns and communities. There was also the arduous work of the Bible women who visited the outlying districts in their towns, knocked on the doors of their neighbors and read portions of the Scriptures to them. It was a matter of daily witness that, like a stone thrown into the water sends out an ever expanding circle of ripples, reaches ever widening circles. In the case of Argentina, Carlos Casares, Pehuajó, Santa Rosa, and Bragado were centers where the missionaries located, but the ever expanding wave of the Gospel was the result of the daily activity of Argentine families who were members of these central congregations. In these early stages of organized evangelization and the institutional shaping of the church, North American missionaries played an important role, but with the passing of time local leaders emerged and assumed the leadership roles in the congregations that were being formed.

Mennonite churches that emerged under indigenous leadership

In places like Alta Verapaz in Guatemala where biological relationships and the formation of clans that included extended families prevail, Mennonite church growth has been rapid. When a prominent member of a family confessed faith in Jesus Christ, in a short time many more family members came forward to take this step. But here again the essential missionary activity was not undertaken by personnel sent by Mennonite missionary agencies, but by the Kekchis themselves who communicated the Gospel in their own language to other families in the region. Brother Pablo Tzul became the apostle among these indigenous peoples spreading the Gospel in many Kekchi villages such as Cojaj, Sacsi Chivo, Chirukbiquim, Se'hol, Chelac, Sa'sis, San Pablo Chitap, Seq'quixpur, Pocola, Chicak, and many more.[36]

The current organizational structures of the Kekchi-speaking churches, which is a legacy of the mission boards and the legal requirements of the Guatemalan government, did not mean

Kekchi woman, Guatemala. (Jaime Prieto Valladares)

---

[36]See Francisco Bernal, *Historia de la Iglesia Menonita en Guatemala,* 19-26.

necessarily abandoning the fundamental elements of their culture. In these Kekchi-Mennonite congregations one can experience the dynamic presence of the Spirit dancing in the music of the marimbas and the guitars that crowd their meeting halls. The planting of corn is a fundamental element of Mayan culture. Among the Kekchi-Mennonite brothers and sisters there is also present in the sowing of their corn, a spirituality that flows out of their ancestral culture. Whenever a family decides to plant their corn, other families hasten to offer their help. After the brush is cleared away by burning, the fields are ready for planting. The family whose fields are being planted invites their neighbors to join them in feasting, just as their ancestors had. They bless, in God's name, the seed that is about to be planted. After they have shared their sweet chocolate drinks and large corn *tortillas* everybody plants the fields with so much enthusiasm that the tasks are soon finished. Then the party continues with songs and praises to God and the feast is concluded with bowls of turkey soup and corn *tortillas*. This common effort, offered with devotion in thanksgiving to God for the land and the seeds for planting, allows them to share the joy of labor and the blessing of nutrition in a communal festival.[37]

Churches that separated from their mother churches

We can also speak of Anabaptist churches that became independent by separating from a mother church over doctrinal differences or questions of leadership. In Costa Rica we see the example of the Mennonite Church of the "New Covenant." This church grew out of a division that occurred in the "House of Prayer" Mennonite Church in Guadalupe over doctrinal and leadership differences. The leadership of the "House of Prayer" opted to continue along the charismatic-pentecostal lines initiated by their pastor Carlos Ulate, while the families that separated established a congregation they called "The New Covenant" in the city of Moravia. The resulting division,

---

[37]Information based on a personal visit of the author to the Kekchi communities in March 1999.

Kekchi Mennonite church, Guatemala. (Jaime Prieto Valladares)

however, did not impede the new congregation from applying for membership in the Conference of Evangelical Mennonite churches of Costa Rica.

The internal organization of this new congregation is similar to that of the other Mennonite congregations in the country.[38] In its first years, the pastorate was assumed by Mayela and David Diller. When they terminated their service and moved to the United States, a pastoral team was put in place and since that time the pastoral leadership has been assumed by two families. These churches are also marked by their missionary character. As soon as they relocated in a new neighborhood the congregation began to respond to the needs of the surrounding community. This is true, even though some of the members of "The New Covenant" congregation attend by commuting from surrounding cities.

It is very likely that a similar phenomenon has been occurring in other Latin American countries, where new Anabaptist congregations emerge, thanks to the evangelistic efforts of a mother church or due to a separation. In some cases

---

[38]The author's interview with the pastors of the "New Covenant" Mennonite Church, Mayela and David Diller, Guadalupe, San José, Costa Rica, 2001.

these new communities continue their affiliation with the national Anabaptist conference. In other instances they become totally independent without wanting to continue their Anabaptist identity. But there are also those separated Anabaptist communities which in spite of their differences with the authorities of the local Anabaptist conference, want to continue to be a part of the Anabaptist tradition. It would be interesting to analyse further this type of independent Anabaptist community. They are generally small communities with a localized vision that seek greater autonomy in economic questions and missionary efforts, than was available in the larger Anabaptist institution where economic arrangements and missionary strategies were generally inherited from their past.

New forms of evangelization and of community in the large cities

The large cities with their particular characteristics and needs present a challenge calling for new ways of being the church in Latin America. In this section we will mention the ministry of *Amor Viviente* (Living Love) in Honduras, the rise of youth ministries in Curitiba, Brazil, and the case of the *Comité Unido de Misión Anabautista (CUMA)* (United Committee of Anabaptist Mission) in Mexico.

Amor Viviente in Honduras (Central America)

Mennonite organizations like *Amor Viviente* in Honduras represent a contemporary form of ecclesial structures and of communicating the Gospel in Latin America. With their large building seating some 1,500 persons, located in the Godoy section of Tegucigalpa near the access highway to the Toncontin airport, *Amor Viviente* certainly needs to be listed among the principal neo-pentecostal churches of Honduras.[39]

---

[39]This is the classification suggested by Karl Braungart. He did not consider that the origins of this church are to be found in the work of Aaron King, a Mennonite missionary serving under the Eastern Mennonite Board of Missions. Simply taking as his point of departure the organizational

Amor Viviente operates its own radio station known as *"Difusora Cristiana de Radio."* In spite of having a general assembly with representation from a number of congregations of that organization in Honduras, the organization has been headed by pastor René Peñalba. Following the strategies of overseas U. S. missions, *Amor Viviente*, in coordination with Eastern Mennonite Board of Missions, has extended the scope of its work to include the planting of churches in other cities, such as New Orleans in the United States and Alajuela, in Costa Rica.

The dynamic of congregational growth is found in the formation of cells, small groups of 10 to 20 people, under the leadership of one person. All of these groups meet together weekly in corporate worship held in their large assembly hall. Among the leadership groups are the worship coordinators, pastoral counselors, those who work with children, marriage counselors, groups in charge of music and theater, hospital visitation ministry, scholarship committee, and literacy classes. In its Honduran context, *Amor Viviente* does not represent an exception. There are other churches of non-Anabaptist origin which operate in similar ways with similar structures, such as *Vida Abundante, Puerta del Cielo* and *Cenáculo*. Organizations like *Amor Viviente* are sometimes questioned. Why begin work in other countries when there are already Anabaptist organizations present, sharing their testimony there, in light of the fact that needs are so great in Honduras? Why have they not related to the Honduras Mennonite Conference? Where is the peace witness which is so badly needed in Honduras? Why is numerical growth so unilaterally emphasized while fundamental elements of the Anabaptist vision are missing, such as community and commitment to justice and peace? Why has *Amor Viviente* remained separate from Central American Anabaptist organizations such as CAMCA, Mennonite Central Committee, SEMILLA, the Justice and Peace Network which have sought to relate to Anabaptist churches in order to

---

pattern and theology of *Amor Viviente* he has immediately identified it as a neo-pentecostal church. See Karl Braungart, *Heiliger Geist und politische Herrshaft bei den Neofingstlern in Honduras* (Frankfurt am Main: Vervueret Verlag, 1995).

dialogue about social, economic, and political conditions in Central America during the very difficult decades through which they have been living?

New alternatives for work among youth in Curitiba, Brazil

In Brazil we also find similar examples, such as the case of a congregation in Curitiba where brother Juan García began a new ministry among the youth of the city. His ministry had grown so rapidly that the local congregation decided to encourage him to continue the work independently. Juan uses the congregation's physical plant to carry out his program for the rehabilitation and socialization of youth from the drug culture, totally independent of the Curitiba church. They have their own ways of worship and internal organization, very different from a traditional church. There is openness to much more spontaneity, social activities, sports, spiritual retreats, etc., that respond to the needs of the youth. Their music is, of course, very different. These are new attempts to create community in the large cities in response to very specific needs, such as those of youth from the drug culture. There are questions that arise out of experiments such as these. Is it possible to carry out a ministry among youth totally independent of the family units of which they are a part? If the church seeks to build relationships in family units and bridge the generational gap, what will be the result of distancing young people from the older people as well as from the children?

The United Committee for Anabaptist Mission in Mexico

The effort to meet the needs of great metropolitan areas like Mexico City though ministries shared by several Anabaptist mission organizations has also resulted in the emergence of new churches. This is concretely the case of the United Committee for Anabaptist Mission (CUMA) in Mexico. In November 1989, a consultation on evangelization in Mexico City was held with the participation of a number of Mennonite organizations. Out of this meeting there arose a decision to establish a committee made up of representatives from all of the various Mexican

Anabaptist organizations in order to develop a program for planting new churches and preparing leaders.[40] Later CUMA was made up of representatives from the Mexican Conference of Anabaptist churches, Mennonite Central Committee of Mexico, Church and Peace in Mexico, and the Anabaptist Mission Coalition in Mexico.[41]

Jorge Rodriguez (CUMA, Mexico City). (Jaime Prieto Valladares)

In reality CUMA was not a new church, or even a new conference, but a movement organized in order to unify and organize all the different resources for the planting of new congregations and carrying out a holistic ministry in greater Mexico City. In this case it is possible to see how this kind of organization arises out of the initiative of Latin American Anabaptist church leaders but, at the same time, continues to be

---

[40]See *Carta de Estatutos, CUMA* (Mexico, D.F., without date). (ACIEAMM).

[41]This coalition is made up of the following foreign mission agencies: Mennonite Brethren Mission and Service Agencies (MBM-S), General Conference (GC), Mennonite Board of Missions (MBM), Franconia Mennonite Conference (FMC), Mennonite Central Committee (CCM), Eastern Mennonite Board of Missions (EMM) and the Evangelical Mennonite Church (EMC).

dependent on mission boards in the United States for financial help and for missionary personnel.[42]

CUMA was dissolved after nearly a decade of activity. This was due principally to the fact that the mission agencies in North America discontinued their financial aid, and the organization was left without the financial resources to continue. A positive result of this effort was making it possible for CUMA to offer its support to congregations which, since their founding, were related to the Conference of Evangelical Anabaptist-Mennonite churches of Mexico (CIEAMM) as in the cases of *La Iglesia Vida Abundante* (Las Aguilas) and *La Comunidad Cristiana Abba Padre* (Tlapacoya). It also contributed to the founding of new churches such as *La Iglesia Pueblo en Transformacion* located in Colonia Pedregal de San Nicolás,[43] and the new work known as *Palabra de Gozo*,[44] where the missionary pastor from the Domincan Republic, Juana María de la Rosa,[45] served. Again, we see that the most difficult problems had to do with relationships between North and South – finances, theology, and practice. How can we achieve economically independent churches with Latin American Anabaptist leadership?

---

[42]Information taken from CUMA, *Manual, Criterios y Proyección 2001, Por la misión integral en la ciudad de México* (Mexico City, without date). (ACUMA).

[43]An interview recorded by the author with Victor Pedroza, Colonia Pedregal de San Nicolas, Mexico, March 26, 2003.

[44]See the author's interview with Sofía Flores García, Iglesia Palabra de Gozo, Mexico, September 12, 1999.

[45]Juana María de la Rosa was born in the Dominican Republic and is a member of the Mennonite church in that country. Her parents are Leonidas de la Rosa and Hortencia Montero. Juana María has been a member of the Mennonite church since 1968. Since May 1994, she has worked as a missionary under the auspices of CUMA in Mexico. See the author's recorded interview with Juana María de la Rosa, Iglesia Palabra de Gozo, Sunday, September 12, 1999.

Mennonite church in Mexico City. (Jaime Prieto Valladares)

Conclusion

In light of our investigation it is clear that we cannot speak of any one Anabaptist typology which serves to distinguish the missionary work undertaken by the mission boards in the United States and Canada from the mission initiatives developed by the immigrant churches of German origin. The experience of a pilgrim people was not merely a Biblical model to be imitated by the early sixteenth century Anabaptists. It has continued to be a reality in the ongoing pilgrimage out of Europe into Latin America. New Anabaptist forms of church life and organization are emerging in Latin America, but they continue to be, to a certain extent, connected to their roots in historical Anabaptism, mediated through the witness of Latin American immigrant churches and through the work of the foreign mission agencies. It will be necessary to investigate these typologies further in terms of the theology and practice of these churches in Latin America. The enormous difficulties that characterize the Latin American continent are also related to the theological and practical challenges facing the Mennonite church in Latin America. It is urgent that we reflect on this typology with a view to widening and completing the initial efforts that we have shared. Confronting this diversity of models can help us to evaluate our ongoing life and mission on this continent.

2

The Fruitfulness of Oral Tradition in the Construction of Anabaptist History in Latin America: Childhood, Violence and Resistance

Oral History as the Memory of the People of God

The Old Testament contains a collection of narratives that tell of God's self-revelation in Israel's history. The Gospel texts also tell us of God's participation in human history through His Son, Jesus Christ. The Gospels were originally the memories of the various communities of faith, first transmitted orally, and later gathered together in written form. God's revelation not only has its place in history, but it is the religious experience of a people that keeps God's saving actions present in their memory, thereby becoming history. It is in history that humans are bound to God and God to humans. Therefore oral history has been, and continues to be, a part of the memory of God's people. Historians have, for a long time, tended to discount oral traditions in their reconstruction of history. It was thought that a history based on written documents lent credibility to its dates and contents. There was the idea that oral traditions should be depended upon only in those cases where no written documentation was available for the reconstruction of a history.

My work as a historian began with my dependence on written sources. These were to be found primarily in letters and church minutes that were zealously kept over the years by the Mennonite missionaries who came to Costa Rica. The Global Mennonite History project has given me the opportunity to carry out a research that takes seriously oral traditions. After gathering the oral witness of many brothers and sisters in Latin America with the use of a tape recorder, I find that my own faith has been greatly enriched. As I have exercised the academic discipline that work with oral sources requires,[1] I arrived at the conclusion that, in the case of a relatively recent history like that of Latin American Anabaptism, we should not consider oral tradition merely as an instrument, but rather as a living archive that enriches with new sources our efforts to reconstruct our history. It is through the life experiences of the members of its communities and churches and the liturgical celebration of its faith, that we are able to understand the memory of God's people. The many testimonies of faith that I have gathered, sometimes with laughter and sometimes with tears, have challenged me to follow Jesus Christ in the context of the community of faith and in the face of the ethical dilemmas present in our Latin American context.

When we speak of the fruitfulness, or fecundity, of oral traditions we simply want to say that the faith stories shared by people in these communities and churches are what bring life to every historical project of the church. We will never forget the story of the baby Moses, rescued from the murderous clutches of Pharaoh who had ordered the killing of the children, when he was hidden in a basket of reeds. When his cries were heard above the murmur of the waters that flowed down the Nile, he was rescued by the daughter of Pharaoh. Later Moses matured in the desert so that he could eventually lead the Hebrews into freedom (Ex. 2:1-10). In the Gospel story we like to remember the birth of Jesus in a rustic stable, fleeing Palestine by donkey during the darkness of the night in the company of his brokenhearted parents, Mary and Joseph, to escape the massacre of the Hebrew children that filled Rachel and many other Hebrew mothers with tears and sorrow (Mt. 2:1-23). Likewise, through the Latin American oral traditions, gathered in their poems and stories, we hope that we, too, will be enriched by the stories in the lives of the children Benjamín Hugo Luayza and Antonio Mosquera.

---

[1]See Paul Thompson, *La voz del pasado, La historia oral* (Valencia: Ediciones Alfons el Magnánime, Institució Valenciana d'estudis e investigació, 1988), and Guyn Prins, "La historia oral," in *Formas de hacer historia,* ed. Peter Burke (Madrid: Alianza Universidad, 1994).

The Poetry of Benjamín Hugo Luayza

One of the texts that best recovers the Mennonite oral tradition in Latin America is the poetry of a child, Benjamín Hugo Luayza. This child's poetry reflects the pacifist tradition of his father, the Argentine Mennonite pastor Albano Luayza. His poem, *España, qué haces?*, was first recited and written in 1937, in the period immediately preceding the Second World War. A wave of fascism was sweeping over Latin America which sought to counteract the threat to the status quo represented in the revolutionary workers' movement encouraged by the success of Bolshevism in Russia. On September 6, 1930, the government of Yrigoyen was overthrown in a military coup. This marked the beginning of a military dictatorship under the Argentine general José E. Uriburú. From that time forward until 1944 the Argentine economy was organized under the influence of a Creole version of fascist ideology.[2] Behind the poetry of Benjamín Hugo Luayza stood his own family and the entire Mennonite community which had embraced the cause of peace in the midst of an Argentine context characterized by fascist illusions. The writings of his father, Albano Luayza, questioned the Argentine military establishment that, already in 1935, with the support of the Roman Catholic clergy, was bent on carrying out a series of military maneuvers.[3]

The message of Benjamín Hugo Luayza's poem contains at its center a deep concern for the Civil War from which Spain was hemorrhaging massively. And it needs to be understood in light of the fact that many of these families of Spanish and Italian origin had, in a not too distant past, emigrated to Argentina. The poem consists of five stanzas and was recited as follows:

---

[2]See Abelardo Villegas, *Reformismo y revolución en el pensamiento latinoamericano,* Fifth Edition (México: Editorial Siglo XXI, 1980), 200-210.

[3]See Albano Luayza, "Vuelve tu espada," *La Voz Menonita* 4 (April 1935): 11,12,14.

Spain, what are you doing?[4]

Spain, what are you doing?
Don't you see that the men
Who inhabit your rich land
are being shot?
Are you losing your sons,
your beloved children?

Spain, what are you doing?
Don't you see that your children
Are being abandoned
Without father, without mother
Perished are their hopes,
When they needed most
The nurture of their mother?

Spain, what are you doing?
Don't you see that your mothers
are losing their children;
Their children who deserve
their sacred affection?

Spain, what are you doing?
Your children are dying
amidst the outcries of warfare,
What curse roars upon us
and within our borders?

Spain, what are you doing?
Your people are dying
bleeding to death,
Can Spain not attain
the peace of her yesteryears?
Spain, what are you doing?

---

[4]From *La Voz Menonita* 6 (August 1937): 1.

This poem does not mention God, but yet it is charged with enormous theological and pastoral content. The central question has to do with theodicy, with the question of how we face evil. *Spain, what are you doing?* is a question that the people of Spain must face. Its pain and suffering are present in its men who face the firing squads, in its mothers who lose their children, in its children who are abandoned, in its sons who die, in its people who are bleeding to death. The poem is a protest straight from a pacifist heart that repudiates warfare, that repudiates military might as a way to subject its people. *Spain, what are you doing?* is a question that is repeated over and over again, with a view to unveiling the realities that brought about so much pain, the suffering and warfare caused by the Spanish Civil War, lasting all the way from 1936 until the fascist triumph of General Franco in 1939. The figure of evil appears at the end of the fourth stanza as an answer to the insistent question: *Spain, what are you doing?,* with another question: *What curse roars upon us and within our borders?* Evil here appears as a roaring curse that produces suffering and death in the midst of the people.

The poem of this child, Benjamín Hugo Luayza, challenges the cruelty of fascist dictatorships. His poem does not mention the name of God, but God is hidden within the love, the nurture, and the warm affection of a mother. God's presence is hidden in the hungry, in the naked, in the orphans, in the mothers who suffer, in the crying children. The question posed by theodicy, the question of evil and of the presence of a gracious God in human history, runs throughout this poem. Benjamín Hugo Luayza views the Spanish Civil War from the perspective of children and their mothers and therefore, from God's perspective. To his own question, *Spain, what are you doing?,* he responds with a sober litany of men before the firing squad, widowed women, orphaned children, and a people hemorrhaging to death. It is a picture that reminds us of Picasso's masterpiece, *Guérnica.* At the same time Benjamin Hugo Luayza would like to remind us that it is better to follow the God of life than the "roaring curse." The memory of fathers and mothers who lost their beloved children and of girls and boys orphaned at precisely those moments when they most needed the sacred affection and warmth of maternal nurture confronts us with its ethical demands.

In the last stanza of Benjamín Hugo Luayza's poem we also see traces of the Anabaptist legacy that he received from his parents: his deep longing for peace. *Your people are dying, bleeding to death, Can Spain not attain the peace of her yesteryears?* These lines not only express an ardent desire for peace but also remember that there was a time in the past when Spain enjoyed peace. If there was peace in the past, it will be possible to build peace in the present. And, at the same time, peace is a demand: it is only possible to live in peace in a social context in which relationships among the people are fraternal and just.

This poem by Benjamín Hugo Luayza stirred public interest at a local level, when it was published by the local newspaper, *El Heraldo*, in Santa Rosa, Argentina.[5] It also proved useful in creating an incentive to contribute offerings in many Evangelical and Mennonite congregations to alleviate the suffering of many widows, orphans and families affected by the Spanish Civil War.[6] Even today, it is a moving experience to again recite this poem of Benjamín Hugo Luayza. It has been recorded in order to remind us that, as disciples of Jesus, we are called to renounce warfare and to foster peace.

The Gospel of Resistance: The Oral Witness of Antonio Mosquera

One of the most surprising stories to surface in the course of our research on the Mennonites in Latin America comes from the oral testimony of Antonio Mosquera. Here, as he

---

[5]The first time that his poem appeared in written form was in *El Heraldo*, a newspaper published in Santa Rosa, Argentina, on June 10, 1937.

[6]For an account of the itinerary of Baptist pastor, Juan C. Varreto, missionary T. K. Hershey and Pablo Cavadore, who was then the secretary of the Argentine Mennonite Conference, among Mennonite congregations during Holy Week in 1938, to collect offerings see: The minutes of the meeting of the pastors of the Argentine Mennonite Conference held in Santa Rosa, February 25-28, 1938.   (Archives of the Argentine Mennonite Conference).

remembers his past, a person of African descent tells us his story in which two currents merge. There are the really beautiful moments of childhood along the San Juan River in the town of Istmina, located on the Pacific coast of Colombia. But there are also dangerous experiences of resistance in a context marked by the violence produced in the conflict between Liberals and Conservatives as well as the intolerance of the Colombian Catholic Church during the decade of the 1940s.

Antonio Mosquera's ancestry can be traced to the black slaves brought from West Africa to Cartagena and to the Colony of New Granada[7] beginning in the first half of the sixteenth century.[8] In the eighteenth century, families of African origin were settled in stable villages in the Province of Chocó along the Pacific coast. These were mining camps operated by powerful slave traders and merchants. The slave traders and merchants settled in the city of Quibdó and from there they traveled out to supervise the work in the gold mines and their agricultural production. The memories of the last of the slave traders in the Provinces of Nóvita and Citará date back to the first half of the nineteenth century.[9]

The legacy of that history of slavery is reflected even in the name of Antonio Mosquera. During those times of slavery, the names of the slaves were taken away and they received the last name of the slave owner. Don Jacinto Mosquera, born in Anserma, was among the earliest descendants of the Spanish conquerors, Francisco Mosquera y Figueroa and Cristobal Mosquera. He settled in the Chocó, "pacified" the Chocó Indians, and by 1699 was the owner of large mines with large

---

[7]Up until 1862, the geographic area that is today made up of Panama and Colombia was known as *Colonia Nueva Granada*. See "Colombia" in Victor Civita, ed., *Geografía Ilustrada, América do Sul*, Vol. IV (Sao Paulo: April S.A. Cultural e Industrial, 1971), 1077-1096.

[8]Rodolfo Ramón de Roux (Coordinator), *Area de Colombia y Venezuela, Historia General de la Iglesia en América Latina*, vol. VII (Salamanca: Ediciones Sígueme, 1981), 22, 149-150.

[9]Nóvita and Citará were the names by which the modern Province of Chocó was known. See Sergio A. Mosquera, *Memorias de los últimos esclavizadores en Citará. Historia Documental, Serie Ma'mawu*, vol. I (Chocó: Promotora Editorial de Autores Chocoanos, 1996).

crews of enslaved workers. For that reason the last name Mosquera is very common in the Chocó Province. Antonio Mosquera received his name because his enslaved forebears had been owned by the Spanish family of Mosquera. His first name, Antonio, comes from the fact that Catholic children were generally given the name of the saint whose memory, according to the Catholic calendar, was perpetuated on the day of the child's birth.[10]

In light of this historical background, we can readily understand why Antonio was born to an humble and impoverished family. However, his childhood was filled with happy memories on the Chocó coastal plain, rich with its variety and abundance of vegetation thanks to its heavy rains (up to 10,000 mm) and high temperatures (as high as 40° C). All this is reflected, as he recounts the memories of his childhood:

> I was born on the banks of the San Juan River in a village called San Antonio, located near Istmina. I was raised there as a child in a peasant family. I enjoyed playing in the river constantly, paddling my canoe, swimming, fishing, and playing in the village square with other children. We watched the boats go by that carried their cargoes down the river and the motor launches that went upstream, since the river was navigable. There we fished for *barbudo, sábalos, jojorro, sabaleta and charre,* fish that are good for eating and have few bones. I fished when the river was low and also when the water was high and muddy. Where I lived there was an abundance of a kind of fish that we called *guacuco* that live among the rocks. They grow to be as much as 18 inches long and are good for eating. We would begin fishing at six o'clock in the morning and would finish at about three o'clock in the afternoon. We would leave some of the fish at home for our own use and sell the

---

[10]Sergio A. Mosquera, *De esclavizadores y esclavizados en Citará. Ensayo Etno-histórico, Serie Ma'mawu,* vol. II (Chocó: Promotora Editorial de Autores Chocoanos, 1997), 1-45.

rest. With the proceeds we were able to help purchase our notebooks and school clothes.[11]

At the age of six, Antonio learned to know the first Mennonite Brethren missionaries who arrived in Istmina to share the Gospel. Daniel and David Wirche were the first Mennonite Brethren missionaries who arrived in La Cumbre, Cali, in 1945 with the intention of continuing the educational program of a little school established for poor children.[12] The following year, in 1946, missionaries John and Mary Dyck, Annie Dyck, Lillian Schaefer, Mary Schroeder and Kathryn Lentzner arrived. This was during the government of Mariano Ospina (1946-1950), which was characterized by its close relationships to the Catholic Church, the suspension of constitutional guarantees and the declaration of "martial law."[13] The conflict between the conservatives and the liberals grew during those years and brought with it negative implications for the Protestant churches which soon became objects of persecution.

In his childhood encounter with the first Mennonite Brethren missionaries, Antonio Mosquera notes an intermixing of differing cultures and a tense social environment that made it necessary for the missionaries to move about at night in order to carry out their evangelizing activities:

> I was a six-year-old when I met the first missionaries who arrived in Istmina in 1946… I especially remember Miss Anna Dyck. They came to my house to evangelize after dark, bringing with them a gasoline lamp for light. Anna taught us to sing choruses with her accordion and taught Bible stories to the boys and girls using a flannel graph. The sound of the accordion was new for us,

---

[11]Interview with Antonio Mosquera recorded by the author at *Colegio de las Americas Unidas,* Cali, Colombia, Friday, October 1, 1999.

[12]J. J. Toews, *The Mennonite Brethren Mission in Latin America* (Winnipeg: Christian Press, 1975), 86, 226.

[13]Jorge Orlando Melo (Coord.), *Colombia hoy. Perspectivas hacia el Siglo XXI,* 15th amplified edition (Santa Fe de Bogotá: Tercer Mundo Editores, 1997), 103-178.

since they were unknown in that town. We didn't have guitars, either. We only had drums, maracas and charascas. That was why neighbors from the village would gather, too. They came to listen to these strange sounds.[14]

Antonio Mosquera was fascinated by the Bible. He liked to hear the stories of struggle and of conflict, the stories of resistance before being subjected. He himself tells us this with considerable feeling: "Then, as a child, I was fascinated by the stories of Samson, of David when he confronted those lions. It caught my attention when God shut the mouths of the lions to keep them from devouring Daniel's friends. The stories of God opening up the Red Sea and the stories of Jesus feeding the multitudes impacted me greatly. That is the reason I liked to go to Sunday School more than to mass."[15]

In spite of his young age, Antonio Mosquera personally experienced persecution as well as hearing about it. A spiral of violence was increasingly involving liberals and conservatives, Catholics and Protestants, conservative Catholic clergy and communists, peasants and wealthy landowners. In the sociological studies of Fals Borda, in the testimonies reported by Francisco Ordoñez, and in the statistics gathered by Juana B. de Bucana we see clearly how the violence of the period also affected many Protestant churches.[16] The Catholic Church had embarked on a colossal struggle for political power in its attempt to restrict religious liberty. It was easy to understand that liberals, Freemasons, communists, and Protestants were all enemies of the Catholic faith and therefore they must be combatted. Led by certain priests and monks, a popular xenophobia broke out against North American missionaries, as

---

[14]Interview with Antonio Mosquera.

[15]Ibid.

[16]Germán Guzmán Campos, Orlando Fals Borda, Eduardo Umaña Luna, *La violencia en Colombia*, vols. I and II (Bogotá: Ediciones Tercer Mundo, 1962-1964). Francisco Ordóñez, *Historia del cristianismo Evangélico en Colombia* (Medellín: Tipografía Unión, 1956), 300-307, 355-375. Juana B. De Bucana, *La Iglesia Evangélica en Colombia, Una historia* (Santa Fe de Bogotá: Asociación Pro-Cruzada Mundial, 1995), 57-59.

well as a hatred of all Protestantism deemed to be of foreign origin.   Part of a song that North American Mennonite missionaries heard in Anolaima, and probably also in Istmina, contained these words:[17]

Protestants, liars:
Your church is not Christ's;
It comes from Zwingli and Luther
And from Calvin, another minister.

Chorus:
We want no more Protestants,
Who come to Colombia to corrupt;
We want no more Protestants
Who defile our land and our faith.

Hundreds of pastors
Are invading our land,
They are ravaging wolves
Brought in by the stranger.

You don't love the Virgin
The Mother of Christ;
In hell you will languish
With Satan, your father.

The surprise attack by a fanatical Catholic mob on the home of Mennonite missionaries Arthur Keiser and Helena Morrow on December 8, 1950, is an example of the violence unleashed in Colombia during those years.   It also affected other Protestant churches. Mobs, urged on by a priest, attacked with stones and clubs and shouted with all their might, "House of Satan, we don't want the Protestants, we don't want the Protestants." Arthur and Helena, hidden in their house behind

---

[17]Bulletin CEDEC, No. 2, March, 1952, 21-22. Quoted in Juana B. De Bucana, *La Iglesia Evangélico en Colombia*, 138-139.

the windows and the tables that they had prepared for their protection, were able to survive the attack.[18]

As we have seen, the variety and abundance of this oral tradition, as it is shared by persons who lived through these experiences, add new elements at each of these stages of the church's history. The experiences of the child Antonio Mosquera are very important, because generally in these situations it is only the testimony of adults that receives consideration. Antonio also experienced violence in his school because of his religious convictions, and in spite of his tender age, he is a model of Anabaptist resistance. Remembering the difficulties he experienced during his childhood in school in Istmina in 1946, Antonio Mosquera reports:

> At that time public education was in the hands of the Roman Catholic clergy and their influence in the schools was very great. For that reason they began to punish me for my attendance at the meetings of the Mennonite Brethren. It became a regular occurrence for me to be punished every Monday. They kept me in at recess time and forced me to kneel on the floor on toasted grains of corn, while holding my hands high over my head. My teacher saw me practically in tears and exhausted, but he still did not allow me to lower my hands. For that reason I began to skip school to play with my friend Alexander Mosquera on the beach along the river. On one occasion my father, Abraham, whipped me with his belt for skipping school. My mother was more understanding and began to ask me why I was absent from school. I told my mother Ernestina that the punishments that I was receiving at school were making me afraid.[19]

---

[18]See Arthur Keiser, "La casa de Satanás," Anolaima, Cundinamarca, Colombia, December 8, 1950. English translation by Daniel Pedraza Sánchez in *Hechos y crónicas de los Menonitas en Colombia,* Vol. I, Investigación de fuentes, Raul Pedraza A., comp. (Colombia, n. d.)

[19]Interview with Antonio Mosquera.

The attitude of Antonio Mosquera shows us a courage to resist, undoubtedly inherited from his ancestors, enslaved in the mines of the Chocó, but now refreshed by his adherence to an Anabaptist faith with all its demands. The punishments were not mere coincidences but were administered with calculated regularity every Monday. His knees, bearing the weight of his body, rested on the toasted grains of corn. The corn, which makes up the daily food of the families in the Choco, here was turned into an instrument for his torture. And remember, we are talking about the punishment of a six-year-old child. The bodily position that Antonio was forced to assume was that of a religious devotee, kneeling with hands lifted high to heaven and crying out for God's blessing. But in Antonio's case it was a form of flagellation, of punishing the body. In spite of his physical punishment, Antonio resisted. He did not curse his persecutor and he even seems to have held back the tears that came to his eyes.

The teacher, from whom Antonio should have been receiving a better example for him to follow in life, was his persecutor. Here scholastic authority was mediated through the power of the Catholic Church. When the political and religious intolerance persisted, it seemed that everyone must pass under its sway, even those who were children in spite of their tender age. They, too, must submit to the dictates of political and religious authorities. We speak of Antonio as an example of Anabaptist resistance because his words reveal that in spite of the punishment that he was suffering he did not take the initiative to report it to his parents. The cool waters that flowed between the sandy banks of the San Juan River, in the middle of the immense heat of mid-day in Istmina became the source of consolation able to restore the happiness inherent in childhood to Antonio and his friend Alexander. Antonio resisted, and he resisted even the authority of his own father who whipped him with his belt. In the social and cultural contexts of that time the authority of the teacher was reinforced by that of the parents, who saw in the school the only hope for their children's social and economic improvement. Antonio resisted not only the punishment of his teacher, but also that of his father. In Ernestina, Antonio's mother, we see a gesture of affection and understanding. She was able, in time, to understand her son's body language. With her wisdom, she broke through Antonio's silent resistance and became one with him in her caresses and kisses of solidarity. The power of love alone must overcome authoritarianism. Later, as he learned the true motives behind his son's truancy, Abraham decided to talk to John Dyck and had Antonio transferred to the educational center of the Mennonite Brethren in La Cumbre (Cali).

Conclusion

The poems and stories of Benjamín Hugo Luayza and Antonio Mosquera invite us to a sober commitment to denounce injustice and warfare. Their messages point us along the path of a struggle for peace that is fully committed. God speaks to us through the poems and stories of childhood and they fill our lives with resplendent light. They fill us with new inspiration and a deep desire to become promoters of peace and to learn to resist non-violently all injustice. Children also want to have their voices heard and to add their stories of peace and resistance to the innumerable testimonies that make up the historical memory of the people of God. Inasmuch as we are willing to listen to the voices of children in our history as the people of God, we will come to understand the words of Jesus when he prayed saying: "I thank you Father, Lord of heaven and earth, because you have hidden these things from the wise and the intelligent and have revealed them to infants" (Luke 10:21).

3
The Participation of Women in the History of Mennonites in Latin America: The Trans-Atlantic Pilgrimage of Melita Legiehn

Generally it is the participation of men that receives the most attention in relating the history of the church. Most of the books reporting the history of the church have been written by men and the presence of women is overshadowed by the names of men. We should, however recognize the recent efforts of several Latin American women to write the history of the church from their own perspective.[1] We should also mention important contributions being made in Europe, the United States, and Canada to rescue Mennonite women from the cloak of historical invisibility in which they have remained hidden for many years. We could cite as an example the research of Marion Kobelt-Groch on the participation of women during the Peasants' War and the Anabaptist movement of the sixteenth century.[2] Or, the conference of women theologians organized under the auspices of the Mennonite Central Committee in Bluffton, Ohio, on June 23 and 24, 1994, with the excellent contributions of Lois Barrett, Dorothy Jean Weaver, Gayle Gerber Koontz, Mary H. Schertz, Rachel Reesor, Wilma Ann Bailey, and Pamela Klassen.[3] And as a last example, we might mention the excellent historical profile of sixteenth century

---

[1]See, for example, Elisabeth del Carmen Salazar Salazar, *Todas seríamos rainhas: Historia do pentecostalismo chileno na perspectiva da mulher 1909-1935* (São Bernardo do Campo: Universidad Metodista de São Paulo, 1995). Elena Alves de Silva Pinto, *O carisma social nas pastoras metodista: estudo de caso de práctica pastoral em ministerios sociais realizados por un grupo de pastoras formadas no período de 1970-1990* (São Bernardo do Campo: Universidad Metodista de São Paulo, 2002).

[2]Marion Kobelt-Groch, *Aufsässige Töchter Gottes: Frauen im Bauernkrieg und in den Täuferbewegungen* (Frankfurt/New York: Campus Verlag, 1993).

[3]The lectures given by the women at this conference have been published in *Mennonite Quarterly Review* 18:2 (April 1994).

women carefully set forth by C. Arnold Snyder and Linda A. Huebert Hecht.[4]

In order to speak about the participation of Mennonite women in Latin America we will briefly relate the biography of Melita Legiehn, a woman whose ancestors were among those who originated the Mennonite movement in Europe. Melita embodies the life and thought of one of the groups of Mennonite immigrants who settled in 1930 in the Paraguayan Chaco and in the state of Santa Catarina in southern Brazil. Melita Legiehn was an educator and, as such, was a somewhat controversial figure in the story of the Mennonite immigrants of Russian and German origin who settled in South America. Her biography probably illustrates, better than anything else, the role of Mennonite immigrant women who settled in Latin America. When we realize that the Mennonite church in Latin America is heir to an Anabaptist legacy that runs through this stream of Mennonite immigrants of German origin, then Melita represents the strong woman whose feet carried her across the old continent until they arrived in Paraguay and finally established themselves in Brazil.

Melita Legiehn's Historical Background[5]

The historical roots of Melita Legiehn's ancestors are linked to the edicts of Catherine II, the Russian empress (1762-1796), of 1762 and 1763, in which she invited persons from the rest of Europe to settle on large uninhabited tracts of land in her country. Among those who migrated in the next several decades were Mennonites who formed the Chortitza and Molochna

---

[4]C. Arnold Snyder and Linda A. Huebert Hecht, eds., *Profiles of Anabaptist Women: Sixteenth Century Reforming Pioneers* (Waterloo, Ont: Wilfrid Laurier University Press, 1996).

[5]According to the German Mennonite custom when a woman marries she takes her husband's family name. For that reason, during the period of her childhood and youth we speak of Melita Legiehn. Later she becomes Melita Kliewer, and finally, we refer to Melita Nikkel.

colonies in Ukraine.[6] In the late nineteenth and early twentieth centuries, Mennonites, including Melita Legiehn's parents, began to settle in Siberia, some of them along the Trans-Siberian rail line.[7]

Great problems for these Mennonite colonies began with the Bolshevik Revolution of 1917. Melita was born in Omsk on August 30, 1924, in the midst of political upheaval and radical economic changes that the new revolutionary government of Russia was introducing.[8] All the guarantees granted to the Mennonites during the Czarist regime were cancelled and their conflicts with the anti-religionist governments of Lenin (1918-1924) and Stalin (1926-1953) reached their climax.[9] When the Communist Party came into power, the Soviet government took over the Mennonite school in Margenau and the curriculum was adjusted to fit the new educational guide lines.[10] Melita's father, who had been teaching in the school, became unemployed.[11] When the political and economic conditions changed radically and the guarantees given to the Mennonites were revoked,[12] colonists living in the settlements of Omsk, Slavgorod and Pavlodar began to prepare for a move to North and South America.

---

[6]The Molotschna colony in the Ukraine dates from 1804. For this story see Peter Letkemann, "Molochna – 2004: Mennonites and their Neighbors (1804-2004): An International Conference, Zaporizhzhia, June 2-5. 2004," *Mennonite Quarterly Review* 74:1 (January 2005), 109-119. See also "Russia," *Mennonite Encyclopedia* 4:381-393.

[7]Cornelius Krahn, "Siberia," *Mennonite Encyclopedia* 4:517-521.

[8]An interview, recorded by the author, with Melita Legiehn, Curitiba, Brazil, Thursday, December 2, 1999.

[9]Gerhard Hein, "Die Mennonitengemeinden und Siedlungen in Russland und in der Sowjetunion," *Die evangelische Diaspora* 41 (1971): 101-115.

[10]Cornelius Krahn, "Omsk Mennonite Zentralschulen," *Mennonite Encyclopedia* 4:517-521.

[11]Melita Legiehn interview.

[12]The guarantees granted to the Mennonite colonies established in Siberia included, for example, that the 1,443 persons who settled in Slavgorod were granted 58,441 acres of land, given reduced fares, a five-year exemption from taxes, a three-year exemption from government service, a salary of 160 rubles, and land free of taxation. Cornelius Krahn, "Siberia," *Mennonite Encyclopedia* 4:517-521.

Legiehn family: Melita is standing at the center between her grandmother (Maria Lange Legiehn Isaak) and her step-grandfather (Gerhard Isaak). Her parents are standing at right: Luise Isaak Legiehn and Julius Legiehn. (Mennonite Church USA Archives, Bethel College, North Newton, Kansas)

Melita Legiehn and the great flight from the Siberian steppes to Moscow

We speak of the "great flight from Siberia" because many Mennonite families of German origin, overwhelmed by the radical ideological and economic changes initiated by the Bolshevist Revolution, wanted desperately to leave Siberia. There was a massive wave of families leaving Siberia for Moscow with a view to seeking asylum in Canada.

Elements of their thought and ideology, in conflict with the Communist alternatives, played an important role in the way Mennonites interpreted their flight from Russia. However, the interpretative paradigm that came to be accepted with time was the Biblical theme of the Exodus.[13] In their stories and poems

---

[13]The use of the exodus as a Biblical theme for interpreting the Mennonite experience in Russia began to develop after 1917 when some 18,000 Mennonites emigrated from Russia to Canada. See Walter Sawatsky,

the emigrants saw a parallel between the Biblical story of Israel fleeing the domination of Pharaoh and the great flight out of Russia. In the work *Vor den Toren Moskaus* we read the story of Russian police who searched for the organizer of the great flight. An old woman replies: "I can tell you who we have for our guide, but it is really a secret." The police ordered her: "Tell us who it is." And she replies immediately: "It's God, our God. There is no other!"[14]

As she remembered these difficult times as they prepared for flight, and later fled from Siberia, Melita said: "I was five years old when we had to flee Russia. With the coming of Communist rule my father lost his employment as a teacher. I still remember those events. It happened like this. My mother had just baked lots of buns. I asked her. 'Why do we need so many buns?' And I noticed that everybody in the house was talking in an undertone. When there is war… when war is expected, one anticipates that there is going to be scarcity. And that made me afraid."[15]

Due to the flight of so many families, it was nearly impossible to get train tickets for the trip from Siberia to Moscow and the police controls over the sale of tickets intensified.[16] However Melita and her sisters and parents were able to leave Siberia: "One day we left the village and went to Moscow. In Moscow there was a brother of my father living whose name was Friedrich Legiehn. He was a convinced Communist. His wife was Russian. She was a very dear woman. They had no children. He knew that we wanted to leave Russia. But he received us with kindness in his house in Moscow. I remember just one little thing about our encounter with my

---

"Historical Roots of a Post-Gulag Theology for Russian Mennonites," *Mennonite Quarterly Review* 66:2 (April 1992): 149-187.

[14]Gerhard Ratzlaff, ed., *Auf den Spuren der Väter: Eine Jubiläumsschrift der Kolonie Friesland in Ostparaguay 1937-1987* (Asunción, Paraguay: CROMOS S. R. L., 1987), 45.

[15]Melita Legiehn interview.

[16]See the story of Isaak Braun, another of Melita's contemporaries who migrated from Siberia to Moscow, Gerhard Ratzlaff, *Auf den Spuren der Väter*, 39-45.

uncle Friedrich; it was the first time in my life that I had seen an electric light."[17]

Melita commented about those times of great agitation throughout the city because of the enormous group of emigrants who were crowding the streets of Moscow and all of the efforts on the part of the German Embassy in Moscow to arrange for the expatriation of its German citizens:

> In Moscow there were 15,000 persons, largely of German nationality, who wanted to leave, but only 5,000 were able to leave. There was no country that would take us. Canada did not give us the permission that we had earlier counted on. Germany only agreed to grant us temporary and conditional asylum, because they were not able financially to accept immigrants. For that reason permission was slow in coming. Stalin said: 'What do you want? Foreign countries don't want to see the likes of you. Get out of here!' And for that reason he sent 10,000 back to Siberia. Since then, whenever the 25th of December comes around, even when I was a child, in Paraguay, whenever we held a thanksgiving service, I thought to myself, we can really celebrate our liberation, those who are still captives in Siberia … can only keep on crying out to God.[18]

Her thoughts seem buried in the past as she exclaims:

> I remember that it was on the twenty-second of November in 1929 that we received Stalin's permission

---

[17]Melita Legiehn interview.

[18]After Germany lost the Second World War, many of the German colonists were able to emigrate to other countries. During *Perestroika* also many Mennonites fled Siberia. See Horst Gerlach, "The final years of Mennonites in East and West Prussia 1943-1945," *Mennonite Quarterly Review* 66:2 (April 1992): 221-246. As for the many relatives of Melita, they had already perished in Siberian camps. (Interview) About the persecution and the suffering through which many Mennonite families lived during and after the Second World War, as well as their Anabaptist witness in the midst of persecution, see Walter Sawatsky, "Historical Roots of a Post-Gulag Theology."

to leave Russia! On the day that we were to leave Moscow, I remember that my uncle Friedrich Legiehn said to my father: 'Brother, please stay here. Do me the favor of staying. What is happening today in Russia through the Stalinist Revolution are only the birth pangs of a new birth. In time, everything is going to change for the good of the people.' But my father said: 'No, we must go.'[19]

The Mennonite colonies scattered throughout Russia had been the beneficiaries of economic favors during the Czarist regimes.[20] Now the Russian peasant peoples had risen up in revolution calling for radical changes that went much farther than the ethnic privileges granted to colonies like the Mennonites. Melita, like all the emigrants who fled Russia, was unable to analyse the political and social situation in the same terms as her uncle Friedrich Legiehn did. They could not understand the demands of an agrarian revolution that would favor the peasant and the impoverished families at the expense of the immense landholdings possible under the Czars.[21]

Continuing her story, Melita remembers:

---

[19]Melita Legiehn interview.

[20]According to statistics in 1926 some 725,000 hectares belonged to the 50 Mennonite settlements, with a total of 385 villages and approximately 120,000 colonists. Older statistics that included some large land holders reported that twice this much land belonged to the Mennonite colonists. Gerhard Hein, "Die Mennonitengemeinden und Siedlungen in Russland und in der Sowjetunion."

[21]The Mennonite leader Johann Cornies is identified in Mennonite literature as one of the most influential in the relations between the Czarist government and the Mennonite colonies in Russia. He possessed many hectares of land and was even able to rent land to the Russian government. In 1847 he owned 500 horses, 8,000 sheep, and 200 head of cattle. The high point of economic and social development among the Mennonites of Russia came between 1850 and 1920. Mennonites came to control 6% of Russian industrial production, in the manufacture of agricultural machinery, and the processing of their agricultural products. Cornelius J. Dyck, *An Introduction to Mennonite History,* Second Edition (Scottdale, PA: Herald Press, 1987), 164-187. Walter Quiring, "Johann Cornies (1789-1848)," *Mennonite Encyclopedia* 1:716-718.

I have two sisters. An older one named Irma and a younger one named Elsa, who at that time was just two years old. My uncle said at that time: 'Leave Elsa here, you are going to return.' And after that I don't remember anything else ... I only remember that we ran to catch the train. My father took off running and grabbed me with such force that it hurt. Just as we got onto the train, a fat man came along, who wore an undershirt on the outside, with a large fur overcoat and closed the door of the train with a bang. My mother lifted me up and then I don't remember what else happened.[22]

So, on this one-way trip, Melita Legiehn, her sisters, her parents, and many more Mennonite families left Russia. And until this very day, the poems of Louise Nickel have helped that generation of Mennonite emigrants to express in melancholic notes, interwoven with pain, a tearful past and memories of their lost fatherland:[23]

Our Homeland

I have wandered everywhere,
Our old homeland is no more!
My feet have trod on thistles and thorns
And nowhere have I found a word of welcome.

The water rushes along the banks like before
But it sings a new and foreign song,
And as I followed the old familiar path,
I only come upon many scattered graves.

Submerged, lost, forgotten, expired
Is everything bright from my childhood.

---

[22]Melita Legiehn interview.
[23]Harry Loewen, *Road to Freedom, Mennonites Escape the Land of Suffering* (Kitchener, Ont.: Pandora Press, 2000).

For so long the desire of my recollection,
the return to my old homeland tugged at me.

But now I know that memory
Alone can make us old ones young;
It weaves a quiet, blessed thread
Way over to that distant land of our youth.

Once more I look in every direction
The old homeland I cannot find any more.
Slowly the red sky of dusk dims,
The homeland of my youth for me is dead.

Refugees sing "Nun danket alle Gott" upon arrival in Riga, Latvia. (Mennonite Church USA Archives, Bethel College, North Newton, Kansas)

With Melita Legiehn from the German refugee camps to the trans-Atlantic voyage

The emigrants made the long trip from Moscow to Germany by train. Tired and sleepy in the arms of her mother, Melita remembers very little of this episode in her life. From Moscow the train moved to the frontier with Latvia, and as they slowly approached their goal they could hear the sound of the train slowly passing through the Red Gate.[24] According to Melita, her parents experienced a great sense of freedom. The memories of that experience, retained through the years, are still with her as she recalls, "When we arrived I remember that the Red Cross was there. The children all received a chocolate bar. People wearing white capes gave us water to drink, and chocolate."[25]

Early in December of 1929, Melita Legiehn, together with her family and many others among the 4,000 refugees, were sent to refugee camps organized by "Brüder in Not" (Brothers in Need)[26] in Hammerstein (Germany). At Hammerstein the passengers passed through quarantine. During the course of the trip, many children had died because of the strenuous trip or of lung infections. Isaak Braun and his wife lost their newborn twins.[27] Another 1,500 refugees were housed in large six-story buildings in Mölln, Prenzlau, Wandsbeck, and Altona.[28] Thankfulness and joy are the memories that remained etched in Melita's mind as she recalled their arrival in Germany: "When we arrived in Germany we were well received."[29] And that was not only the sentiment of Melita, but of the entire group of emigrants who lived through the experience. Germany was seen as a protective mother, welcoming her children as they fled from Russia.[30]

---

[24]The Red Gate marked the Russian frontier with Latvia. On one side of the Gate is the shape of a cross and on the other the red flag of the Soviet Union. The triangular metal structure under which the train moved holds a star. For a photograph of this structure see Gerhard Ratzlaff, *Auf den Spuren der Väter*, 51.

[25]Ibid.

[26]An organization made up of Red Cross representatives, Catholic *Caritas*, the German Evangelical Church, and Mennonites to care for these refugees fleeing Russia. The president of Germany, Hindenburg, heeded the call by contributing fifty thousand German marks toward this cause. Harold S. Bender, "Brüder in Not," *Mennonite Encyclopedia* 1:445.

[27]Gerhard Ratzlaff, *Auf den Spuren der Väter*, 39-45.

[28]Christian Neff, "Refugee Camps," *Mennonite Encyclopedia* 4:270.

[29]Melita Legiehn interview.

[30]Concerning this feeling see *50 Jahre Kolonie Fernheim: Ein Beitrag in der Enktwicklung Paraguays* (Filadelfia, Chaco, Paraguay: Jubilaeumskomitee, 1980), 17.

The stay in Germany was short. Families received medical examinations by Canadian doctors. Some families became separated because only some of the family members were allowed into Canada. In fact, very few families were accepted by Canadian immigration officials. Furthermore, news came that Brazilian authorities were insisting on stiff health requirements at ports of entry, raising the specter of emigrants being returned to Germany.[31] For these reasons Paraguay became the alternate destination for Melita and her sisters and parents, as well as for many other emigrant families. These families sailed from the ports of Hamburg and Bremen for their long voyage across the

Refugee group at Mölln, Germany, who went on the fourth transport to Paraguay. (Mennonite Church USA Archives, Bethel College, North Newton, Kansas)

Atlantic before arriving in Buenos Aires. In Buenos Aires the refugees transferred to a small steam ship for their trip up the rivers to Puerto Casado in Paraguay.[32]

---

[31]"Wie es zur Auswanderung der Mennoniten nach Paraguay kam," *Bibel und Pflug,* March 12, 1955; quoted in Gerhard Ratzlaff, *Auf den Spuren der Väter,* 61-64.

[32]*50 Jahre Kolonie Fernheim,* 6.

Melita Legiehn in the burning heat of the Paraguayan Chaco

The Fernheim Colony in the Paraguayan Chaco was established on April 26, 1930, for the purpose of receiving the immigrants from Russia and Siberia. The large group of Mennonite emigrants from Russia, of which Melita and her family were a part, had been in Germany, temporarily, in the hopes of receiving the visas that would permit them to enter Canada. When the Canadian government denied the request of Benjamin H. Unruh in Karlsruhe, Germany, the Mennonite Central Committee met on January 25, 1930, to investigate the possibility of sending these emigrants to the Paraguayan Chaco. The original plan called for a total of 374 families, made up of

Menno Colony residents waiting at Kilometer 145 in the Chaco to pick up the third transport of Russian Mennonites. (Mennonite Church USA Archives, Bethel College, North Newton, Kansas)

1,853 persons. The first of these family groups left the refugee camp in Mölln for Paraguay on January 25, 1930. Other groups followed them until a total of eight groups of families had been moved. The travel costs and other financial needs had been met by German authorities and the Mennonite Central Committee.

In Paraguay, MCC negotiated with one company to purchase the land on which to settle these families.[33]

This 1930 group of Russian emigrants traveled from Puerto Casado to the last station on the railway, known as Kilometer 145, and from there on, in large ox carts, they followed the roads that the Mennonites who had founded the Menno Colony had cleared through the Chaco.[34] The last stage of their trip took them six days since it ran through patches of jungle, prairie pasture lands, underbrush and cactus and all this with temperatures ranging between 35 and 45 degrees centigrade.[35] The contrast between the hot climate of Paraguay, compared to the extreme cold of the Siberian steppes, opened Melita's eyes to the fact that they were now on a new continent.

> Today the Chaco is a large colony, but at that time there were many more trees. It was a jungle with valleys full of cactus. That's where we built our first houses, it was very, ... very difficult. The climate was very hot and it was not easy. In Siberia it was the opposite, terribly cold. My grandmother, who always accompanied our family cried, saying: 'Children, we can't have Christmas here... there is no snow. ...' I remember that I cried, my grandmother could not be happy at Christmas time because there was no snow.[36]

In 1932 still more emigrants from Harbin (China) arrived in the Fernheim Colony which by now had adopted a Russian community form of social organization.[37]

---

[33]Cornelius J. Dyck, "Fernheim Colony," *Mennonite Encyclopedia*, 2:323-324.

[34]Gerhard Ratzlaff, *La ruta Transchaco: Proyecto y Ejecución: Una perspectiva Menonita* (Asunción, Paraguay: 1999), 20-33.

[35]Nicolai Wiebe, Gerhard Isaak, and others, "Schreiben aus Paraguay an die mennonitische Weltkonferenz," in Gerhard Ratzlaff, *Auf den Spuren der Väter*, 70-75.

[36]Melita Legiehn interview.

[37]Gerhard Ratzlaff, *Ein Leib, viele Glieder: Die Mennonitischen Gemeinden in Paraguay* (Asunción, Paraguay: Gemeindekomitee, Asociación Evangélica Menonita del Paraguay, 2001), 71.

Melita Legiehn and the National Socialist Movement

During their pilgrimage in Russia, the Mennonites had become accustomed to building and operating their own schools. Once they had settled in the Fernheim Colony in the Chaco, the first thing they did after building their church was to prepare a place for their children's school. Under the heat of a burning sun, and in the shade of a spreading tree, with hammers in hand, they built their first little school. The Mennonite emigrants organized their educational system based on six years of elementary instruction and four years of secondary school. The central school in Fernheim was organized in 1931 in the village of Schönwiese at the initiative of Wilhelm Klassen, Fritz Kliewer and Melita's father, Julius Legiehn. Here she finished her primary studies.

Melita received from her parents her interest in education, politics, the church, and literature. In 1936 the school was transferred to Filadelfia, the principal center of the Fernheim Colony.[38] Here Melita finished her studies. With the election of her father, Julius Legiehn, as *Oberschulze* (senior administrator) of the colony in 1938 and the euphoric return of Dr. Fritz Kliewer[39] from the Germany of Adolf Hitler[40] in 1939, the colony increasingly began to experience the influence of

---

[38]Waldo D. Hiebert, "Fernheim Zentralschule," *Mennonite Encyclopedia*, 2:326-327.

[39]Fritz Kliewer arrived in Germany in 1936 and remained there until 1939 during the period when Adolf Hitler's program as chancellor of the Third Reich was at its peak. He lived through the boycott initiated against the Jews by Hitler's government. He also witnessed the formation of the "German Christian Movement" that formed around Ludwig Müller, an army chaplain who was named by Hitler as "Bishop of the Reich."

[40]Already in his political platform of February 24, 1920, Adolf Hitler had announced, "I believe that it is my duty to do the work of the Almighty Creator: By combating the Jews, I am doing the Lord's work.... If we were to divide the human race into three categories – founders, conservers and destroyers of culture – only the Aryan branch could be considered representative of the first category." Adolf Hitler, *Mi Lucha*, trans. Alberto Saldivar P. (Santiago de Chile: Ediciones "Más allá", n. d.), 22, 85.

National Socialism.[41] Melita was no exception to this movement, since her own father promoted it among the youth and at the same time she was an admiring student of Dr. Fritz Kliewer and his wife, Margarete Dyck, also a teacher.[42]

It is difficult to imagine how families like the Kliewers and the Legiehns, whose historical roots were in the Mennonite tradition, would set aside their Anabaptist principles in order to embrace the ideals of National Socialism. National Socialism was marked by a racist ideology as well as aspirations of world domination carried out by armed force. Among the results of these actions were the Holocaust and the outbreak of the Second World War. At this period in the life of Melita there was a clear contradiction between an Anabaptist faith that stresses non-violence and the values of the Kingdom of God and the ends sought by National Socialism, which affirmed "Aryan" racial superiority and the use of armed force to obtain power. Many questions about the thought and actions of Melita Legiehn during this period remain buried in her silence.

Nicolai Wiebe, a leader in the denomination known as the *Allianzgemeinde* (Evangelical Mennonite Brethren) stood up in opposition to Legiehn and Kliewer, because he thought that they were moving the community toward a total identification with the ideology of the National Socialists. In the words of Fernheim leaders like Jakob Siemens, Heinrich Pauls and Abram Loewen, the solidarity of many Mennonites with the ideology of National Socialism was tied to their past. They affirmed: "We know, and we give thanks for it, that God created National Socialism in a time of great Bolshevik danger in Western Europe. The Almighty God has made the Führer Adolf Hitler a great blessing to many nations and we trust that

---

[41]Julius Legiehn served as *Oberschulze* from 1938 to 1944. *50 Jahre Kolonie Fernheim*, 60, 179.

[42]Beginning in 1933, Julius Legiehn and Fritz Kliewer had been placed in charge of work among the youth. *50 Jahre Kolonie Fernheim*, 120.

Fernheim Colony meeting hall with picture of Adolf Hitler at the front. (Mennonite Church USA Archives, Bethel College, North Newton, Kansas)

He will preserve for many years our beloved fatherland."[43] When the North American missionaries in Argentina: Nelson Litwiller, Elvin V. Snyder (Canadians) and Josephus W. Shank (U. S. citizen) visited the colony in April of 1940 they were scandalized when they discovered that the colony celebrated the birthday of Adolf Hitler.[44] The Mennonite Central Committee played an important role in the resolution of this conflict in the Chaco.

Two other events played an important role in undoing the National Socialist movement among the Mennonite immigrants: a) In 1942 the government of the Paraguayan dictator General Higinio Morínigo, in spite of the fact that internally it continued to be fascinated by this fascist current, broke off diplomatic relations with Italy, Japan, and Germany.[45] b) On the other hand, a dangerous epidemic of typhoid fever broke out in the

---

[43]Jakob Siemens, Heinrich Pauls, and Abram Loewen to B. H. Unruh, September 29, 1937, "Paraguay, Fernheim Colony 1937," Hist. MSS. IX-6-3, AMC, quoted in John D. Thiesen, *Mennonite and Nazi? Attitudes among Mennonite Colonists in Latin America 1933-1945* (Kitchener: Pandora Press, 1999), 82.

[44]John D. Thiesen, *Mennonite and Nazi?*, 132-134.

[45]Pablo Gonzalez Casanova, ed., *América Latina: Historia de medio siglo,* Volume I, South America, third edition (Mexico: Siglo XXI, 1983), 356-357.

Chaco in 1943, taking the lives of entire families. Margarete Dyck, the wife of Kliewer, contracted the disease and died, leaving their three children orphans. Melita described these difficult times in the following manner:

> At that time we were still living in tents. At the end of 1943 I was outside of school when I heard Margarete say to her husband, 'I don't know what is happening to me, I have such a bad headache'. She died of typhoid fever at Christmas time in 1943. The funeral was held on December 25, 1943. I was her student. She had an excellent knowledge of literature, and I liked literature very much. I kept on attending school with the one who would later become my husband. She knew ahead of time that she was going to die. One time she said to her husband: 'Listen. I know that I am going to die. But who will be the mother of my children?' Her husband was a very optimistic person and he said to his wife: 'Dear, you are not going to die.' And she responded, 'Yes, I feel sort of like a candle that is dying out. Listen to me as I tell you who is going to be mother of my children. When I die, please marry Melita Legiehn.' (One can imagine how difficult this was for the one who was going to be my husband!) And then she died. The oldest child was 5 ½, the second was 4, and the third was just over one year old. She had married when she was a little older. She was older than her husband and their three children were her great joy. She had been a great source of encouragement to her children because at that time life was hard in the Chaco. It wasn't like it is today. There was no air-conditioning. But the children ... she worshiped them. She had cared immensely about her children. Later my husband said, 'well, I need to get married again'. My husband was 19 years older than I was. He knew my parents and they were great friends. Naturally, he was my teacher in school. But he did not know my personal life. I was 19 years old. I don't remember having any special friend. It was wonderful to feel the way I did. I had friends, but

I had never been in love. Even today, I don't know why it turned out this way. I was interested in politics and in literature ... but had never been in love. And then, all at once, I was united to him. Then he talked with me. My sister had said to me one time: 'I have the intuition that you are going to be the mother of those three children.' I said to my husband, the one who had been my teacher, yes. This was difficult for my mother. She was beside herself. She said to me: 'Melita, you can't do this. Can't you understand?' And she said to Fritz: 'Fritz, Melita doesn't know how to cook. She has never learned how. And she doesn't know how to keep house, either.' But Fritz, the eternal optimist that he was, said: 'That's not a problem. She can learn how to do it.' Well, 'I said to him: Yes.'[46]

With Melita's marriage to Fritz Kliewer the life stories converge of two people from Siberia and Prussia with difficult experiences during the Communist Revolution, going through the emigration to Latin America, accustomed to patriarchal social organization, with traditional church rules and hopes tied to the ideology of National Socialism. On May 11, 1944, the Kliewer and Legiehn families were expelled from the Fernheim Colony after the Mennonite Brethren congregation passed a resolution condemning the National Socialist movement, due to its incompatibility with Anabaptist principles.[47]

---

[46]Melita Legiehn interview.

[47]For details related to the tensions and the surprising unraveling of the National Socialist movement in the Fernheim Colony, in addition to the literature already cited, see the following: Peter Klassen, *Die deutsch-völkische Zeit in der Kolonie Fernheim, Chaco, Paraguay 1933-1945: Ein Beitrag zur Geschichte der auslandsdeutschen Mennoniten während des Dritten Reiches* (Bolanden-Weierhof: Mennonitischer Geschichtsverein, 1990); Gerhard Reimer, "The Green Hell Becomes Home: Mennonites in Paraguay as Described in the Writings of Peter Klassen," *Mennonite Quarterly Review* 76:4 (October 2002): 221-246.

Melita Kliewer's next stage in Asunción, Paraguay

The next stage in the lives of Melita and Fritz Kliewer and their children is set in Asunción, Paraguay. A number of Mennonite families were already living in Asunción. Since October 1931, Peter and Grete Fast, who arrived with other Russian emigrants aboard the steamship "Toro," had been living in Asunción. Asunción had become a transit center for Mennonite families and for a number of young persons from the Mennonite colonies in Paraguay who were finishing their studies. The Fast home had become a place of meeting among the Mennonite emigrants for celebrating their faith. When Melita and Fritz Kliewer arrived in Asunción they related to several Mennonite families already living in the city. This was in 1944, just as the Mennonite Central Committee was opening offices to give aid to Mennonite families. In 1947 there was a new influx of Russian emigrants and it was decided, with the help of the Mennonite Central Committee, to organize a Mennonite congregation in Asunción. The committee charged with giving the initial impulse to the formation of a faith community in 1949 was made up of preacher Ernst Harder, Peter Unger, David Thiessen, Kornelius Walde, and Fritz Kliewer.[48]

Concerning her experiences in Asunción Melita says: "We went through a difficult time in Asunción. Fritz worked in the Goethe School in Asunción. Meanwhile, we had five children, since his children from his previous marriage lived with me. Then we established a home for students (*Schulerheim)* in Asunción. I was in charge of the administration. My husband taught at the Goethe School and at night offered classes at our student home. Both of us worked very hard. We didn't have an opportunity to purchase our own house."[49]

Through the periodical *Mennonitische Welt*, published in Winnipeg, Melita and Fritz learned that in Brazil the Mennonite colonies located in the state of Santa Catarina wished to build a school. Melita commented on this: "We then discovered

---

[48]Gerhard Ratzlaff, *Ein Leib, viele Glieder*, 85-91.
[49]Melita Legiehn interview.

common interests. We were looking for a home for our children and they needed teachers. Fritz traveled to Brazil and visited the recently established Witmarsum Colony, observing everything. When he returned he said: 'It is beautiful there and the climate is temperate. You are going to feel good there. And there we can own our own land.' My husband and I had written our own reading books for the Mennonite schools in Asunción and with that material in hand we left for Brazil towards the end of 1952."[50]

Melita Kliewer's Arrival at New Witmarsum in Brazil

On March 27, 1951, seventy-seven members of the old Witmarsum Colony in the Krauel Valley, under the leadership of Peter Pauls, announced that they were going to build a new Witmarsum on the Cancela Ranch in Palmeira, Paraná. Thus, as other families from the Krauel Valley moved to states further south in Brazil, establishing "Colonia Nova," these families moved northward to build a new Witmarsum. The tensions among the different Mennonite denominations in the Krauel Valley were resolved as those who formed Colonia Nova were Mennonite Brethren, while the others moved to the new Witmarsum. On the matter of community organization we note in Colonia Nova increased freedom from traditional forms, while in Witmarsum the organizational structures continued to be more centralized.

For Melita Legiehn and Fritz Kliewer, Witmarsum represented a new opportunity for them in the context of this new colony to exercise leadership in the emerging educational program. Accustomed as they were to exercising leadership in centrally structured communities, Witmarsum offered them a newly opened door to develop their family and community projects in the new socio-political context that was beginning to emerge in Brazil, leaving behind them those ideological tensions of the Second World War era.

---

[50]Melita Legiehn interview.

New Witmarsum was built on the lands of the Cancela ranch, with an area of some 7,800 hectares in the state of Paraná. It was agreed that each colonist would be given 10 hectares for agricultural use while the rest would be reserved for common pastures for raising cattle. None of the colonists were actually given title to their lands. The purpose was to strengthen cooperation among the colonists and guarantee the colony's privacy. Colonists were not free to sell their properties or settle on new lands without the colony's permission. In this way the colony was able to continue the traditional structures they had inherited from the Mennonite colonies in Russia.

Men drawing lots for home sites in village 4, Witmarsum, Paraná, 1959. (Mennonite Church USA Archives, Bethel College, North Newton, Kansas)

In the course of their move from the Krauel Valley to their new settlement, New Witmarsum, some of these families decided to remain in Curitiba. The main group was joined by another 20 families from Paraguay. Among these were Melita and her husband Fritz Kliewer and their children. Two years after the establishment of New Witmarsum there were a total of 74 families totaling 455 persons. In contrast to what happened at Colonia Nova, in Witmarsum there have been fewer families who have deserted the colony by the end of the decade by moving to Canada, Germany, or returning to Paraguay in times of economic crisis.

By the end of 1952, Melita and her family had moved from Paraguay to remain permanently located in Witmarsum, Brazil, the final stage of their long pilgrimage. Melita Legiehn described the arrival of her family in Witmarsum as follows: "Finally, we got through the last gate and were able to travel along the street in Witmarsum. Would it be in village number 1? On the right, some distance away, we could make out the neighborhood. The houses came into view. Witmarsum, Paraná, at that time was only one year old. The ox carts were parked in front of a small building in the center of the colony. We got out. A sister, dressed in white, ran to receive us. It was so good to feel at home! Then someone approached us to make us welcome. It was the Elder, Johannes Janzen ... We were very tired. The children quickly found places to spend the night. Then my husband called me to the door and said: 'Come over here and listen to the melodious murmur of the brook.' 'Yes, I can hear it. And what is it murmuring to us? Happiness? Suffering?' The future is in God's hands."[51]

Fritz Kliewer was named educational director for the colony of Witmarsum and Melita Legiehn, together with Elfriede Loewen, Abram Kröker, Marlene Krahn, and Hans Janzen were chosen as teachers.[52] In a letter from Fritz Kliewer, addressed to Walter Quiring in Canada in March of 1953, he commented: "The enrollment in the Witmarsum school is very good, 42 students in primary school (Volksschule), and 31 in secondary

---

[51]The original puts it this way. "Es dämmert schon, als wir durch das letzte Tor und dann auf der Witmarsumer Strasse fahren, zuerst durch Dorf Nr. 1. Recht weitläufig sah es nach aus. Man sah ab und an ein Haus oder einen Schuppen. Witmarsum in Paraná war ja noch nur ein Jahr alt. Der Wagen hält vor einem kleinen Haus im Zentrum der Kolonie. Wir steigen aus. Eine Schwester in weisser Tracht kommt auf uns zu. Wie mich das angenehm berührt. ... Und dann steht noch jemand da und heisst uns wilkommen. Ältester Johannes Janzen ... Wir sind sehr müde. Die Kinder finden schnell ein Nachtlager. Dann ruft mich mein Mann vor die Tür. 'Komm, hör mal, wie schön der Bach rauscht.' 'Ja, ich höre es ... Und was rauscht er uns? Freude? Leid?' Alle Zukunft stehet bei Gott." Melita Kliewer, *Bibel und Pflug*, Nr. 4, 1958.

[52]Peter P. Klassen, *Die russlanddeutschen Mennoniten in Brasilien, Band II. Siedlungen Gruppen und Gemeinden in der Zerstreuung* (Bolanden Weierhof: Mennonitischer Geschichtsverein e.V., 1998), 223.

(Mittelschule), without counting the children who are still in the Krauel and will be arriving in the coming months."[53]

Melita Kliewer's Contribution to Education in New Witmarsum

When Melita arrived in Witmarsum, she realized that a new stage in her life was beginning related to the colony's educational program. As she was showing the pictures of the first school in New Witmarsum she commented: "And in this way we began to rebuild our lives in Brazil. My husband was in charge of beginning an educational program. This is where my husband taught the children. It was in this simple building that the school was begun. Back then we were just beginning with the basics."[54]

The other project on which Melita spent a lot of time and energy was the new periodical, *Bibel und Pflug*. This is how she described it. "Fritz' long standing dream had been to begin a periodical, and that's what we did when we began the *Bibel und Pflug*. ... In this building my husband began the periodical. Here we received all our correspondence. We began this periodical in 1954."[55] *Bibel und Pflug* appeared for the first time with a design drawn by Hans Legiehn. It was a Bible with a cross over it, and to one side there was plow opening a furrow. The *Bibel und Pflug* was published under the control of an editorial board consisting of Dr. Fritz Kliewer, Dr. J. S. Postma, Johannes Janzen, David Nikkel, Julius Legiehn, and Peter Klassen. Its purpose was stated as follows: "The Bible is the foundation of our religious life and the plow is symbol of our work and culture – not merely agriculture – in all the world. We seek to be plowmen,

---

[53]Letter from Fritz Kliewer to Walter Quiring in Canada, Witmarsum, March 15, 1953, quoted in Peter P. Klassen, *Die russlanddeutschen Mennoniten in Brasilien,* Band II, 224.

[54]Melita Legiehn interview.

[55]Ibid.

who through our work in the cultural context of the countries in which we are active, will be a blessing and a service."[56]

By this time Melita Legiehn had to assume responsibility for all of the household tasks, and as secretary she was in charge of transcribing all the materials and reproducing them using the primitive techniques available at that time.[57] This made her work very difficult. With perspiration dripping from her brow, we catch a glimpse of Melita the woman, busy with the daily responsibilities of caring for a household full of children and meeting the deadlines of a periodical that had been the dream of her husband. "I even came to hate that periodical for all the work it demanded of me. Meanwhile we had six children. But my husband was happy to be able to share widely the events and the pulse of the Mennonite community."[58] We will pick up the story of the on-going development of *Bibel und Pflug* later, but not before recognizing the importance of Melita Legiehn's role in publishing this periodical in which the life and culture of the Mennonite community was reported and conserved.

Melita's life took a new and totally unexpected turn when, in June of 1956, Dr. Fritz Kliewer died of a heart attack at the age of 51. He had just returned from attending a Mennonite church Conference in Uruguay. "This came as a severe blow to the Mennonite community here, because he was the school teacher in Witmarsum. And *Bibel und Pflug* needed to go out very soon. But in reality nobody is totally indispensable. Soon others came forward to fill those roles. I worked for many years on that periodical, the *Bibel und Pflug*. I also worked in the school. And for many more years I taught in the Kindergarten (*Vorschule*) and I did it with enthusiasm."[59]

---

[56]*Bibel und Pflug*, No. 1, 1958, quoted in Peter P. Klassen, *Die russlanddeutschen Mennoniten in Brasilien.* Band II, 250-251.

[57]Ibid.

[58]Melita Legiehn interview.

[59]Ibid.

Melita Kliewer meets up with an angel on earth

The sudden death of Fritz Kliewer radically changed the life of Melita Legiehn. Now it became necessary to assume the roles of both father and mother, to love, to care for, and to support their six children. In addition to raising her husband's children from his previous marriage, she also had Hartmuth, Gerd Uwe, and Friedrich Wolfgang, the children of her marriage to Fritz Kliewer. With the death of her husband she had to take upon herself the administration of their farm, look after their dairy and milk production, and care for the pigs as well as the crops.

At this new stage in her pilgrimage the story of her friendship with a young woman named Lena is the most striking. Lena was, for Melita, like an angel come down from heaven to the earth! When Melita remembers Lena her eyes light up and she says happily, "We have angels here on earth. Of this I am absolutely convinced. And among those angels who have been sent to me in my times of greatest need, one of those was Lena, a peasant girl from the vicinity. She decided to help me with the farm work. Lena worked for me for seven long years. She worked as if the land were her own. She taught me to plant, to feed the hens, and to care for the cattle. And I am never going to forget it."[60] The totally unselfish solidarity on the part of Lena for Melita Kliewer at that difficult junction in her life is one of the most tender moments of Melita's pilgrimage. Melita saw in Lena the providence of God when she exclaimed: "I will never forget that angel sent to me from God. A simple woman, a peasant girl. She was very strong. Lena had her own parents and siblings. At the beginning, we scarcely knew each other, but she wanted to help me. She came from a large family. But she didn't want to live at home because of her strong and dominating character. Lena always receives a Christmas present from me because I am so grateful to her. I gave her my former husband's ring. I couldn't repay her with money for all the work she had done for me during those seven years. Then one day some time later, I saw her again, and she was still wearing the

---

[60]Ibid.

ring that I had given her. That was a sign to me that she did appreciate my gratitude."[61]

Melita's marriage to David Nikkel (1967)

The marriage in 1967 of Melita to David Nikkel, one of the most respected leaders in the Witmarsum Colony, marked a new stage in her pilgrimage. In her own words she reported: "After 11 years I was about to be married again. It was difficult for me. But the children were grown and well. Hartmuth had gone to Germany to work for Volkswagen. He had married there. He is a very intelligent man. He finished secondary school here. Then he continued with his university studies. After that he completed a doctorate in theology at Marburg. He married a member of the Evangelical Lutheran Church. All my children are good. I married again in December of 1967. My new husband was a farmer named David Nikkel. At that time he was 24 years older than I."[62]

David Nikkel was a farmer who already in Russia had begun to demonstrate his gifts as a preacher. Together with Peter Pauls, they became pioneer leaders of the first Mennonite colony in the Krauel River Valley. And together they were able to envision on the horizon the need to form new Mennonite colonies. New Witmarsum, with the passing of time, became a mother colony that contributed to the spread of Mennonites in Brazil. In the same history in which Melita made so many contributions to education and culture, David Nikkel had contributed to the conservation and the re-creation of Mennonite colony structures. David Nikkel had for many years been an elder, pastor and preacher in Witmarsum. When he married Melita he was already retired, but he continued to preach in the congregation.

---

[61]Ibid.
[62]Ibid.

Shaped in a patriarchal community,[63] beginning with her home in Siberia, and then moving through Fernheim, in Paraguay, and finally upon her arrival in Witmarsum, in Brazil, in one way or another, Melita was always close to key people in the areas of the educational, religious, and cultural life of the Mennonite colonies. When she was asked why she married men who were so much older than she was, Melita laughed and said: "I didn't have time. I was always busy with my children. My children were the most important to me. I often suffered from my solitude. And sometimes I thought how nice it would be to again be caressed and kissed by a man. But I was always deep in my solitude and committed to caring for the children. And I had known my new husband for a long time. He was well known here in the community. He was a very intelligent man. His wife had died and he had always shown appreciation for me. It was strange. I can understand that for him it must have been terrible to know that he was 24 years older than I. But I was sure that God had spoken clearly to me. And I didn't want to. And I didn't want to. David Nikkel confessed his love and asked me: 'I love you. And I also know that I am much older than you are.' I knew that I had to make some decision and I answered. 'No.' And so he would understand that I meant no, with the help of my son, we built a big house. But later, one evening I broke down. And I said, 'God, I want to be obedient. I'll follow your path.' My children, who by that time had their own families, said: 'Mother, you shouldn't live alone all the time, and that David Nikkel is going to take good care of you.' He had a large family. He had 12 children. My daughter worked as a

---

[63]Mennonite communities were organized in such a way that the person in charge of organizational and political matters was always a man. The person in charge of educational programs in the colonies was a man. The elders and the pastors were men. And finally, in the internal structures of family life in the colonies, authority was always exercised by the husband. There are differences in the ways in which power and authority are perceived in Mennonite families in closed ethnic communities and perceptions held in present-day middle class North American society. For a recent study of power and authority in Mennonite families in the United States see J. Howard Kauffman, "Power and Authority in Mennonite Families," *Mennonite Quarterly Review* 68:4 (October 1994), 500-523.

teacher. So finally I remarried. I went to live [with him] in [his] pretty village. And my daughter continued her work as a teacher in our school."

Certainly there was a big difference between the ages of Melita and David Nikkel. But at the same time, they had both been born in Siberia. They had worked together in publishing *Bibel und Pflug*. They shared in common the religious and community life of Witmarsum. We ask ourselves, how is it that Melita was able to accept the traditional community norms by which the well-being of a man, already advanced in years, is given priority over the intimate wishes of a younger woman to find love? Without a doubt, it was the image of David Nikkel as a religious leader in the community for so many years that played an important role in Melita's coming around to seeing his will as the will of God. The story of Melita shows us a woman willing to forgo her own personal well-being in deference to the demands of a patriarchal community. As a mother she did not withhold any efforts to do the very best for her children. Referring to her life with David Nikkel, Melita said, "One day after we had married he said to me, 'What is yours belongs to your children. And here is what belongs to my children. So I am going to build a house for you. I have a piece of land and we'll build it there. He had two single children who were still living at home.' So he said, 'each of these will get a nice room of their own in the new house.' So he built a big house. We saved and saved. And each of the children had their own room. We also had a spare room for visitors. I and my husband understood each other well. Shortly after we were married he began to suffer from diabetes. His illness did not cause me much trouble. I enjoyed his friendship so much. He was very kind to me and to my children. And my children were amazed that we were able to get along with each other so well."[64]

In the environment of the Mennonite community, where the roles of women and men are so distinct, David Nikkel as pastor exercised spiritual control, but Melita in her food preparation provided new alternatives in the process of conserving

---

[64]Ibid.

Mennonite identity.[65] The kitchen and the flower and vegetable gardens became holy places where the woman was able to break through the dichotomies established by rigid family structures. If Lena was the angel who appeared at an earlier stage to care for the garden in a time of great solitude, Melita, with her considerable culinary creativity, was the one who now prepared the food, the salads, and the cakes which delighted the whole family. Melita thought that the nicest thing about her marriage to David Nikkel happened when every Saturday their house was filled with the visits they received from their children from both marriages.[66] So Melita's creative imagination which she had inherited from her mother expressed itself in the bread she baked, in the delicious meals and the salads she prepared, using fruits, legumes, and other products from all the various places that her pilgrimage had taken her. Each weekend, her table was transformed into the very best place to worship God with thanksgiving, to share the culinary treats Melita had prepared, and to tell each other their life stories in order to strengthen their common identity.

Remembering David Nikkel's final goodbye, Melita recalled his all-embracing spirituality: "He was a spiritual man.… After eight and one-half years my new husband suffered a stroke and died.… He said to me, just before he died in peace: "I have preached the Word of God for 40 years. But do you know what it means to love God? When do we love God? Only when we love other persons. We can't hold onto God in our grasp. … Only by loving our neighbor, can we love God. Tonight I am thinking about the people I have known, and I believe I have loved them. That's the way I can love God." And Melita echoed the same great truth when she said: "I believe that this is the way it is. I cannot say that I love God without loving my neighbor. It just isn't possible."

---

[65]On the role of women in the construction of Mennonite identity see Pamela Klassen, "What's Bre(a)d in the Bone: The Bodily Heritage of Mennonite Women," *Mennonite Quarterly Review* 68:2 (April 1994), 229-247.

[66]Melita Legiehn interview.

Melita Nikkel, Promoter and Protector of German Mennonite Culture

Melita was a participant in the destinies of her emigrant community from the time they fled Siberia, passing through Moscow, Germany, and the Paraguayan Chaco until they finally settled in Witmarsum, in Brazil. In her cultural contributions one notes not only her capacity to conserve positive elements from the past, but also to participate in the innovations that the Witmarsum Mennonite colony experienced in their efforts to respond to the needs of children and poor families in their Brazilian context by sharing their culture and serving.[67] Through their periodical, the *Bibel und Pflug,* they were able to overcome the tensions between the Mennonite Brethren and the Mennonite churches during the decades of the 1960s and 1970s and redefine its objectives accordingly. The beginnings of dialogue between the two conferences that were initiated in the 1970s bore their fruits in the 80's, when both organizations were able to work conjointly through this medium for sharing news from their communities and churches in the Brazilian context.[68]

Through her writings Melita has continued to promote her people's culture. She publicized the production of dolls (*Strohpuppen)* that Esther Prochnau-Penner and her family had initiated. The family developed this business, which consists of the production and distribution of Brazilian peasant dolls made from corn husks. Melita Legiehn's reporting of this activity resulted in the quite considerable growth of this modest enterprise. These dolls were offered to the public during the Witmarsum Colony's Jubilee celebration in 1980. Before long they received an order from São Paulo and production was increased. Then a representative of the Brazilian government's official program for the promotion of the work of artisans

---

[67]For details of the service work of the Mennonites in Brazilian society through the *Associação Menonita de Asistência Social* (AMAS) and the *Associação Menonita Beneficiente* see *Die russlanddeutschen Mennoniten in Brasilien,* Band II, 348-358.

[68]Ibid., 248-253.

(*Programa Nosso)* showed interest and today thousands of these dolls are sold every year. Esther Prochnau-Penner, the creator of these dolls, won first prize in the state-wide expositions of nativity scenes in 1992 and 1994.[69]

Another of Melita's reports on the artisanship of Boris Janzen in Witmarsum was also influential. Janzen is a furniture maker by profession and produces lamps of various kinds and shapes, rustic hand-carved corner-nooks (*Bauernecken mit Schnitzwerk),* and bedroom and kitchen furniture. His artistic creations have reached far beyond the boundaries of Witmarsum and are currently being produced for export to other countries.[70]

In 1989, when the community in Witmarsum decided to convert the home of the former owners of Cancela Ranch into a small museum, Melita, who has come to be known as a specialist in Mennonite culture, was called upon to organize the archives and serve as their custodian. In 1991, on the occasion of the forty-year celebration of the *Cooperativa Mista Agropecuaria Witmarsum Ltda,* Melita Legiehn and Horst Gunther Kliewer presented an album of black and white photographs with historical captions in both German and Portuguese covering the forty years of history of the Mennonite colony of Witmarsum. In the second volume of his monumental work featuring detailed historical research on the Mennonites in Brazil, historian Peter P. Klassen expressed his gratitude to Melita Legiehn for her custodial care of the archives and her dedication to investigating and reporting on the relationship between the conserved documents and the historical events they reflect.[71]

Reflecting on her long pilgrimage Melita says: "My destiny was already determined. There are two possibilities in relation to one's destiny: a) To love your destiny. At any rate, you have no other choice. b) To love your destiny. This is what God has chosen for your life. I understand other choices, but I believe that the second is most appropriate for me. I love my destiny. It's what God has chosen for my life. It gives me joy as I reflect

---

[69]Ibid., 264-265.
[70]Ibid., 264-265.
[71]Ibid., 9.

on what has been my destiny. There have been many difficulties, but every human being experiences difficulties in life. I once heard a sermon that I will never forget. The pastor said: 'Every boat carries its cargo below. And that cargo serves a good purpose, because the boat needs it. In the same way every human being carries his/her own load of difficulties. I am happy. All my children have married and have their own families. My own children have given me 9 grandchildren. But I also have many more grandchildren through the children of my husbands. I have experienced the love of my children."[72]

Conclusion

The truly notable role of Melita Legiehn in the pilgrimage of the Russo-German emigrants from the old continent to Latin America tells us that the history of the church can also be told from the perspective of women. Melita's little body, held in the grasp of her father in their flight from Moscow, sometimes visibly broken by the patriarchal requirements of her community, perspiring and wasting away in her love for her children, comes to us as an example of the many women who today are in a struggle for their livelihood as well as for the livelihood of their families. Melita's life also questions our home life and challenges us to form relationships characterized by more dialogue and mutual responsibility among family members. The difficult National Socialist stage of Melita's life also alerts us to the question of our own identity. A truly Anabaptist identity should most definitely question all exclusive ethnic identities. One of the fundamental challenges that faces us is how to be faithful to God and to the values of God's reign of justice in the context of our ethnic identities. Melita tells us that true solidarity, especially the kind that is experienced among women, is an act of mutual tenderness in the midst of a world dominated by a male mentality that prizes the possession of power. In Melita we see an effort to remember the history of one's community, and to give new meaning to the spiritual

[72]Melita Legiehn interview.

contributions and cultural efforts of the Mennonites within a modern and changing society such as that of Brazil today. Melita also teaches us that, in reality, we can only love God inasmuch as we love our neighbor.

With this brief biography of Melita Legiehin we want to point out the importance of writing our Mennonite history from the perspective of women. We still have a lot to learn from her life, but we hope that this brief contribution will encourage others to keep on writing her story, as well as that of many other Anabaptist women in Latin America. We recognize our enormous theoretical limitations in that we cannot always keep up to date with the very considerable body of literature that has been written in recent years on the themes of gender, sexuality, family life, anthropology, and oral history. It is an enormous challenge to create a history from oral traditions and the interdisciplinary task of the sciences, but stories like that of Melita Legiehn encourage us to continue. Since her life story is so closely tied to our Latin American contexts, it raises many questions about the life and mission of the Mennonite church in Latin America. Her life is intertwined with those of many other women, children, men, elderly, youth, and families who struggle for their livelihood on our continent. Along the innumerable paths that Mennonite communities scattered all across Latin America tread today, we may well come across Melita's footsteps.

4
Missiology and Anabaptist Ecclesiology: Challenges to Building Peace

Introduction

When we speak of missiology, ecclesiology, and theological education from the perspective of our institutions and churches we need to view them as exercises in understanding the mysteries of God. We can only begin to speak of God inasmuch as we are willing to perceive God in the infinite greatness of the Cosmos, in the immensity of God's loving kindness as manifest in the Son, Jesus of Nazareth,[1] and in the manner by which we express ourselves – in our educational centers, in our churches, in our diverse cultures, in our society – with deeds and words reflecting the love of God that dwells in our hearts.

When we think of missiology we must go all the way back to the creation of all things because the glory of God is manifest there. When we speak of ecclesiology we must immediately fall back on the Holy Scriptures because they witness to God's covenant with humanity. It is a covenant that extends from the formation of a people, Israel, passing through the New Testament, with the coming of Jesus, to the full manifestation of God's Holy Spirit reaching to all nations and cultures.

We are gathered here in a center of theological education and it is possible that we are thinking of the Biblical sciences, of hermeneutics, of systematic theology, of anthropology, of the Biblical languages, of the pastoral disciplines, of the history of the Church, of ethics, and of other disciplines as the basic avenues through which to reflect on the missiological and ecclesiological issues of our time. Now I grant that there is a degree of truth in this, but on this occasion I would like to begin to think about the missiological and ecclesiological challenges before us by referring to the revelation that the loving God shared with me through our sister Cecilia Espinoza Jiménez, a sister from the indigenous Trique people I visited in March 2005.

---

[1]Robert Haight, *Jesús símbolo de Deus* (São Paulo: Editora Paulinas, 2003).

Cecilia Espinoza. (Jaime Prieto Valladares)

Cecilia Espinoza lives in the town of San Isidro de Morelos, in the district of Tlaxiaco in the state of Oaxaca, Mexico.[2] It is located about 300 miles southeast of Mexico City. She is descended from a people that during the colonial period had as their authorities persons of considerable note and whose positions were hereditary. During the nineteenth century, thanks to the confiscation of lands carried out during the agrarian reform, the lands of the Trique were sold to the García Veyrán Company. However, following the Revolution, a part of their territory was restored to the Trique people. From 1920 onward several groups of the dominant Putla people entered the Trique territories as coffee buyers and dealers in arms and rum. Between 1940 and 1948, San Andrés Chicahuaxtla and San Juan Copala were reduced from their status as municipalities, with only San Martin Itunyoso remaining as a municipality.[3]

---

[2]The Trique people are found in the western part of the state of Oaxaca, principally in the following localities: a) San Andrés Chicahuaxtla and Santo Domingo del Estado, a district of Putla; b) San Martín Itunyoso and San José Xoxhixtlán, in the district of Tlaxiaco; and c) San Juan and San Miguel Copala in the district of Juxtlahuaca. For more details see: "Triquis/Tinujei", http://www.aquioaxaca.com/nuevo/index.php?option=com_content&task=view&id=217

[3]Ibid.

Church in La Laguna de Guadalupe. (Jaime Prieto Valladares)

Throughout the lowlands the traditional structures of authority among the Trique disappeared because the cultivation of coffee tended to increase the private ownership of property and violent conflicts over the possession of land increased. In San Isidro de Morclos, as well as in La Laguna de Guadalupe located in the highlands, conflict over the possession of land was much less frequent. But the scarcity of land led to the migration of its inhabitants toward the small cities nearby and even to the larger cities farther away in search of work. For these reasons, Cecilia Espinoza is part of an indigenous people that has struggled for many years to survive in the midst of a society that marginalizes its indigenous cultures.

The women weave their own garments and proudly wear them in La Laguna de Guadalupe and San Isidro de Morelos, as a part of their cultural heritage handed down to them by their grandmothers. Today their textiles not only are an external expression of their indigenous identity, but also by selling them they are able to support their families. Mothers and daughters rise early in the morning to grind corn on their handmade stone mills[4] and travel to the nearby municipal markets to sell their *tortillas* and *tamales*.[5] After they lost their land, the men have not always been able to find employment. Mexico City has absorbed many of the Trique emigrants by offering them the tasks that no one else will perform. This has led to depression and alcoholism among many.[6]

The day I visited with Cecilia Espinoza she was lying in bed, with her long dark hair, and without her lower limbs. She greeted me with a broad smile. I found her living in a hut with walls of sticks plastered with mud and a dirt floor. Her humble hut stands beside the building where the *Pentecostés Montes de Sion* congregation meets. Her father lives nearby in another simple dwelling. Across the street there is pasture. Here her brother, Fernando, lives with his wife, Alejandra, and their daughters in a little house surrounded by dogs, chickens, turkeys, and a goat.

While we were talking, Fernando and Cecilia's elderly father approached us, dressed in simple clothing, barefoot, and carrying a walking cane in his hand. He greeted me in Trique and I soon realized that he was hard of hearing.

When Cecilia began speaking in her native Trique language I, of course, could not understand her, but her brother Fernando translated her words into Spanish. Cecilia's words sounded to me like the soft murmur of fresh water that flows in their

Pentecostés Montes de Sión. (Jaime Prieto Valladares)

---

[4]A stone for grinding corn widely used among indigenous peoples in Central America.

[5]An interview recorded by the author with Alejandra Bautista Sánchez, San Isidro de Morelos, Oaxaca, México.

[6]An interview recorded by the author with Fernando Espinoza Jiménez, San Isidro de Morelos, Oaxaca, México, Thursday, March 3, 2005.

highland streams. As Cecilia was recounting her story she described a dream, a vision that she had received that made my hair stand on end and my heart beat faster. As she was speaking I remembered the words of the prophet Joel (2:28): "Then afterward, I will pour out my spirit on all flesh; your sons and daughters shall prophesy, your old men shall dream dreams, and your young men shall see visions."

Cecilia Espinoza's Vision

I dreamed that I was being lifted into the heavens and that my feet were dangling freely. In my hands I had the Holy Scriptures that shone like the sun. I dreamt that I was reading from the Holy Scriptures. There was the story of that star-filled night when the Lord Jesus of Nazareth said to Nicodemus: "God loved the world so much that he gave his only Son, in order that all who believe in him should not perish, but have everlasting life" (John 3:16). Another of the favorite texts that she read was the confession of longsuffering Job: "Naked I came from my mother's womb, and naked I shall return there, the Lord gave, and the Lord has taken away; blessed be the name of the Lord" (Job 1:21).

In my vision it sometimes seemed that the earth was opening with terrifying rumbling and quakes. People ran from one place to another, crying out in great fear. But I stood there calmly with the Word in my hand, lifted up toward heaven with my feet dangling freely below me. I shared the Word with them and told them not to fear, because God was with them.

These words reached my people, and the enormous multitude formed itself into a circle. They came carrying their children in their scarves. The women came dressed in their red *guipiles* (garments) with their multi-colored needle work. I kept reading the Word and it came alive among the vast crowd of people who kept looking up and listening to the stories of *Yan'anjan*[7] the Creator God and the gentle work of Jesus through his parables and miracles.

The people were harvesting their corn and the *nopal*[8] that serves them as food and medicine. The flocks of donkeys, goats, and sheep covered the hills around La Laguna and the water in the rivers flowed with great turbulence around the enormous circle of people that joyfully listened to the words of wisdom coming from the Word of Life as I read. We were all filled with overflowing happiness. And many other peoples, anxious to hear these life-giving words gathered around the circle.[9]

Trique women. (Jaime Prieto Valladares)

---

[7]This word refers to God the Creator among the Trique. It is the same word that it used in the Trique translation of the Bible.

[8]A type of cactus that grows in the vicinity of San Isidro de Morelos.

[9]This is a free version of the author's interview with Cecilia Espinoza, with a Spanish translation from the Trique language by Fernando Espinoza, San Isidro de Morelos, Oaxaca, México, Friday, March 4, 2005.

Pastoral care

Cecilia's vision leads us to consider the challenge not only of preaching the Gospel, but also the importance of pastoral care with a view to making people whole in our communities, in our congregations, and in the neighborhoods in which we share our faith. We often need other mirrors in order to discern and evaluate the ways in which we carry out our mission and shape our ecclesiologies. The theological vision of Cecilia Espinoza enables us not only to catch a glimpse of the relationship between heaven and earth, but also to see the spirituality that flows from the Word and the daily struggle for survival of our indigenous peoples, people of African descent, and people of mixed race. Cecilia's vision alerts us to the necessity of caring for our planet, buffeted by warfare, by the destruction of the environment, and by unbridled human consumption of its resources. Cecilia's testimony and vision allow us to perceive not only the utopian dimension of heaven within our limited earthly context in which the struggle for personal and collective existence takes place, but also as the context for pastoral care by which we can touch the woes of our world with truly pastoral healing.

The pastoral care of our co-workers, our communities of faith, our peoples, the marginalized in our city slums, emigrants and victims of violence, our own bodies, our families, nature and our ecosystems, must be the point of departure for the academic task.[10] When we speak of pastoral care we must recall other terms in our language such as care of souls, ministry of accompaniment, group ministries, pastoral care within a culture, pastoral care in time of grief, of sickness and of death. The theological task, seen as reflection on and as a systematization of our understanding of God, must be undertaken with

---

[10]For recent materials on "pastoral care" see Julio de Santa Ana, *Por las sendas del mundo caminando hacia el reino* (San José: DEI-UBL, 1984); Howard Clinebel, *Asesoramiento y cuidado pastoral* (Michigan: Libros Desafío, 1999); Leonardo Boff, *Saber cuidar: ético do humano – compaixão pela terra* (Petrópolis: Editora Vozes, 2004).

tenderness, affection, concern for, and knowledge of how to care for others.[11]

Cecilia's theological vision was preceded by an expression of pastoral care characterized by tenderness and concern. Coming as she did from a very humble background in a poor indigenous Trique family, Cecilia began to experience medical problems with her legs. At eight years of age, she suffered from a disease that left her legs paralyzed and finally it was necessary to amputate them. Years later, in 1977, Claude Good, a Mennonite Voluntary Service worker, visited her. In addition to visiting her, he provided her with medicines and vaccinations.[12] Claude and his wife Alice Good and their daughters had arrived in Mexico early in 1960 to live in La Laguna de Guadalupe, a small town near San Isidro de Morelos.[13] They also worked at translating the Bible into the Trique language. Claude kept on visiting Cecilia in her illness for a considerable period of time without talking to her about God. But after some time, Cecilia, intrigued by the gentleness and compassion of Claude, wanted to know about his understanding of God. In that way, with the help of the New Testament that had been recently (1966) translated into Trique,[14] Cecilia began to learn the message of Jesus Christ.

By using the Trique translation of the New Testament, Cecilia Espinoza learned to write and to read the Bible in her own language. In San Isidro de Morelos, Cecilia became key to the spread of the Bible's message among her own people and in their own language. The way in which she went about sharing the Biblical message was this: her family gathered around her,

---

[11]On the theologial task see Sidney Rooy (Comp.), *CLADE IV, Presencia cristiana en el mundo académico* (Buenos Aires: Ediciones Kairos, 2001).

[12]On the origins of Mennonite mission work in Mexico see Kenneth Seitz and Guillermo Zúñiga, "History of the Evangelical Mennonite Church of the Central Plateau of Mexico," unpublished manuscript, 1976. (Shared with the author by Guillermo Zúñiga.)

[13]On the beginnings of the Mennonite work among the Trique in La Laguna see interview with Pascual Salazar García, recorded by the author, La Laguna, Oaxaca, Mexico, Saturday, March 5, 2005.

[14]See: "Nuguan' naca nagui' yaj yya Yan'anj and an nga" in *El Nuevo Testamento de nuestro Señor Jesucristo.* (México D. F.: Sociedad Bíblica de México, Texto en Castellano 1966; Sociedades Bíblicas en America Latina. Trique de Chicahuaxtla y Español, 1963).

and seated in her wheel chair, she would tell the stories of the Old and New Testaments in Trique. Then the leader or pastor of the Triques would teach from the texts that she had read, adding further comments on the reading. This went on for many years since, even though Trique was the native tongue spoken by all, they were unable to write or read in their own language.

One of the texts that had embedded itself deeply in Cecilia's heart was Mark 16:15:[15]

The Gospel of Mark 16:15

Trique	English
Hue dan ni gataja so' Guni'. Nej si, Guij y re' Gacha' xumigui ga' ui' nuguna' an Re'nuguan sa' a rian daran' gui.	And he said to them, Go into all the world and proclaim the good news to the whole creation.

This beautiful text reminds us of our Anabaptist tradition expressed in the preaching of the Austrian evangelist Hans Hut in the sixteenth century of the Gospel to every creature.[16] In the first place, this was Jesus' charge, to preach the good news in all of the world and in every language to the creatures who inhabit every geographic region of the earth. In the second place, we must recognize God's manifestation in all of nature, since its central message is God's revelation to every creature and in every creature; that is, to every creature in whom God has breathed the breath of life. In the third place, the text contains

---

[15]"Nuguan' naca nagui' yaj yya Yan'anj anj an nga," 341.

[16]Hans Hut was one of the most effective of the Anabaptist evangelists in Moravia in his response to this text. Hans Hut, together with other martyrs, was burned to death in his cell in 1527, following the Augsburg Anabaptist Synod. Herbert Klassen, "The Life and Teaching of Hans Hut (Part I)," *Mennonite Quarterly Review* 33:3 (July 1959), 171-205.

the notion that creation not only reveals the Creator, but also the divine desire that God's will be revealed to all creation.

The Great Commission in Mark's Gospel (16:15) takes on a special dimension when we remember that the text has an imperative, "Go", and the one who recites it and accepts its authority for her life has no feet for going. In spite of her physical limitations, due to the loss of her limbs and her poverty, Cecilia is a lovely example of how God can use any of us in service. With her hands she not only has woven beautiful multicolored garments in the tradition of her ancestors, but they have handled over and over the Biblical texts. This is what her brother Fernando pointed out when he said, "My sister Cecilia has read and shared the gospel so continuously with so many people that she has in recent years worn out three New Testaments. She is actually using her fourth New Testament."[17]

Today we marvel at Cecilia's theological vision, but we need to reiterate that it is only with pastoral gentleness that we can grow in our deep desire to share God's great good news with students, professors, lay people, pastors, and members of our churches. By this we do not intend to attenuate the role of academia in our understanding of reality through the social sciences, economics, hermeneutics, or the study of the Biblical languages, or semiotics, but that these must all be subordinated to our capacity for compassionate caring. Without this, without that pastoral gentleness, we pastors as God's creatures will not be able to fully proclaim the will of God to our fellow humans.

The vision from heaven: God's caring and human pain

Cecilia's life is so surprising because, without any formal education and in spite of the poverty in which she has lived right up to the present, she was the key person, together with her brother Cornelio Espinoza, Pascual Salazar García, Isidro Salazar García and Claude Good, who made it possible to

---

[17]From an interview with Fernando Espinoza.

translate and publish, in 1984, a version of the Old Testament,[18] called Si-Nuguan' Yan'anj Xangá.

Returning to her vision, we note two dimensions, that of heaven and that of the earth. In her vision she found herself in the heavenly plane where she had recovered the limbs that she lost in childhood. She was the one who had the Word of God in her hands to proclaim its message to surrounding peoples. What I find astonishing in her vision's heavenly dimension is that when she opened the Word for the first time it was to remind all of God's unlimited kindness and great love, loving us to the point of being willing to send his only Son in order that we might have fullness of life, eternal life. The first textbook with which Cecilia learned to read in her own Trique language was the New Testament.

From 1977, when Cecilia Espinoza first began to read and to understand the Gospel of our Lord Jesus Christ in Trique, until 1984 when she collaborated on the first abbreviated edition of the Old Testament in Trique, the stories that her people heard from Cecilia's lips were of, and about, Jesus. We can say that Cecilia, moved by the mercy of God and by her reading of the New Testament, came to understand, just as the Apostle Paul[19] and Menno Simons[20] had, that Jesus Christ is the foundation of incarnation and the dazzling grace of God toward all humanity and creation. The stories of Jesus found their way deep into her

---

[18] *Si-Nuguan' Yan'anj Xangá, Resúmen del Antiguo Testamento en Trique de Chicahuaxtla y en español,* First Edition (W.H.B.L. Liga del Sembrador A.C., published for the American Bible Society, 1984).

[19] I Corinthians 3:11: "For no one can lay any foundation other than the one that has been laid; that foundation is Jesus Christ." (NRSV)

[20] The foundational writing of Menno Simons bears the title, *"Dat Fundament des Christelycken leers"* and was first published in 1539-40. It should be pointed out that for both, Jesus Christ is the foundation for faith, Menno Simons in the context of a medieval hermeneutic that emphasized following Jesus in the light of God's wrath, and Cecilia in her vision that emphasizes the kindness and gentleness of God. On the concept of discipleship in Menno, see Marjan Blok, "Discipleship in Menno Simons' Dat Fundament: An Exercise in Anabaptist Theology", in Gerald R. Brunk, *Menno Simons: A Reappraisal: Essays in honor of Irvin B. Horst on the 450th Anniversary of the Fundamentboek* (Harrisonburg, Virginia: Eastern Mennonite College, 1992), 103-129.

heart, above all because the Gospel shows us the great love of the Son of God, Jesus of Nazareth, who walked along the paths of Galilee teaching the Gospel of the Kingdom, healing all manner of diseases among the people. Cecilia Espinoza came to know Jesus of Nazareth, and she identified with the one whose fame spread throughout all Syria. And the Holy Scriptures tell us that they brought to him all who were afflicted with disease and all sorts of sickness, the demon possessed, lunatics, epileptics, and paralytics (Mat. 4:23-25).

Her second reading of the Word is no less impressive. Cecilia identified with Job, the patient sufferer of the Old Testament. The text of Job 1:21, written by her very hands in the Trique language, takes on deep significance. "Naked I came from my mother's womb, and naked I shall return there; the Lord gave and the Lord has taken away; blessed be the name of the Lord." In the first part of the text we find hidden the existential agony that Cecilia Espinoza suffered for many years–her childhood, her birth into a large poverty-stricken family. We note that Cecilia, just as Job had done, recognized that life proceeds from God. Life's greatest miracle is life itself. But Cecilia experienced physical pain in her body, and just as Job had, she remembers the fragility of life. "A mortal, born of woman, few of days and full of trouble, comes up like a flower and withers, flees like a shadow and does not last" (Job 14:1-2).

In her memory there were the difficult years of childhood brought on by the extreme pain in her limbs. She recalls sleepless nights, the throbbing pain in her legs that racked her little body. She remembers the blankets on her bed, damp with perspiration from her fevers and hot tears. She recalls peeking through the cracks in the walls of the hut as she watched the neighbor children feeding grains of corn to the chickens. Why must I suffer so, while my brothers and sisters run after the butterflies among the wild flowers? How much, oh God, would I like to play without pain! How much, oh God, would I like to run with the other little girls in the neighborhood! These were the questions and the exclamations, ever present in Cecilia's life, that led her to identify with the suffering of Job.

Cecilia's years of physical prostration bring to mind, just like Job, our pain and our diseases and the fragility of our own lives.

Storms and hurricanes tear off the roofs, destroy our crops, blow down the trees, ruin the levees, and take their toll of victims. There are times in our lives when disease comes and pain lays our loved ones low, when they and sometimes we lose a member of our body. There are special moments in our lives when disease attacks, leaving us wounded and hurting. Death also comes unexpectedly and sometimes snatches away those with whom we have shared our lives and love for so many years. Right now we can remember our pain and suffering at the loss of loved ones. We remember family members and friends, sick and wasted by the human fragility we all share. In our seminaries and theological institutions, in our communities, and in our churches we need to remember to care for one another. I speak of an attitude that must arise out of the depths of our hearts causing us to show kindness in response to the loving gentleness of God.

Our institutions of learning should be able to help us better interpret Job's text with the help of the Hebrew. Good biblical and theological commentaries may help us to understand better the debates over the themes of retribution and the meaning of evil, or to better analyze the figure of the Leviathan. Sciences such as psychology help us develop techniques for counseling and caring for the sick and grieving. But first we must allow the Holy Spirit to put on us the seal of gentleness, moving us to compassion and solidarity with the suffering.

In Latin America we carry out our theological reflection and pastoral care in a context characterized by the discouragement of our youth, violence toward our children,[21] women, and the elderly, social and economic injustices, premature deaths, and the spread of AIDS, natural catastrophes, the destruction of the

---

[21]In Brazil every four minutes a person is wounded by firearms, every 15 minutes a person dies as the result of firearms. In the state of Rio de Janeiro alone in the year 2004, a total of 6,438 persons died as the victims of firearms. Many of the dead are young persons and children. This led the Brazilian government to call for a popular referendum on October 23, 2005, in order for the people themselves to decide if arms and munitions sales should be prohibited in Brazil. See Chico Octavio e Elenilce Bottari, "Uma morte a cada 15 minutos," *O Globo*, year LXXXI, no. 26,347, Sunday, September 25, 2005, 18-20.

natural environment, the increase of disease in epidemic proportions, and accidents of all kinds. For this reason I have emphasized the heavenly dimension of Cecilia's vision and the challenge to be kind and gentle toward others, just as God is with us.

The vision from the earth: Earthquakes and tempests

The second dimension of Cecilia's vision revealed what was happening to those who are below. The first thing that catches our attention is the terror and fear that takes hold of people because of the earthquakes, opening up wide cracks in the earth. I think that Cecilia's vision has much to tell us about the realities of our time as we experience natural disasters happening one after another. Hurricane Mitch went through Central America in the decade of the 1990s leaving the area completely destroyed, with the resulting economic setback still being felt in a region which was already poverty stricken. Later, El Salvador was impacted by an earthquake that displaced many poor families in 2001. In recent years Jamaica, Cuba, and other parts of the Caribbean have been devastated by hurricanes, torrential rains, and tidal waves. The images of devastation caused by the tsunami in December 2004 are still fresh in our minds. Whole towns were destroyed in Asia and we still don't know just how many perished from this catastrophe.

The hurricanes Katrina and Rita are the most recent of these catastrophic events to affect North Americans. Without pity they wiped out large areas in New Orleans and left cities along the Mississippi coastal area devastated. Areas in Texas and Louisiana were also seriously affected. While U. S troops were occupying the city of Baghdad, people of African and Hispanic descent waited in desperation in the midst of their ruined houses and businesses, hoping that helicopters and medical personnel might come to their rescue. People ran about filled with fear and terror in the devastated city of New Orleans, just as Cecilia had seen in her vision. All nature is reacting to the great climate changes brought on by humanity's warfare, destruction of forests, contamination of the environment, and the break-up of the protective layer of ozone. Just like the text in Romans says, it seems that the whole creation is groaning with labor pains, awaiting our liberation (8:22-23).

Earthquakes and hurricanes destroy everything in their paths, but they also reveal the injustices of those governments that have never been interested in conserving the ecological equilibrium, nor for the welfare of the impoverished people of their nations. Interested more in keeping its troops in the occupied cities of Iraq, Bush's government was indifferent in the face of Katrina, even knowing ahead of time what would happen. And not only that–the suspicions of the parents of black soldiers who fight the wars dictated by Washington soon surfaced. When they were most in need of understanding and help, they were being left behind by a nation preoccupied with its wild dash to prosperity. It is like the *New York Times* reporter recalled, just as it was with the sinking of the *Titanic*–the richest and the most powerful were the ones who were the first to be saved.[22] In her first vision, Cecilia saw terrified people crying out and running from one place to another. Widespread terror and outcries were also a part of the tragic scenes emanating from the city devastated by Katrina. The hurricane force winds destroyed everything in their path. Shopkeepers with guns in their hands kept potential thieves from ransacking their stores. Children were pictured wading among scattered objects in their homes. Streets filled with up to six feet of water were turned into lakes. Youths roamed the streets carrying with them merchandise taken from the flooded stores. Thousands of homeless persons crowded into the Superdome and the Convention Center. The refugees reported that soldiers were shooting at innocent youths. The call-up of 50,000 reservists to protect private property from pillaging and restore a semblance of order in the midst of the chaos came late.[23] As Thomas Hobbes had written in 1651 in his book *Leviathan,* the absence of the authority of the State leads to the breakup of society, leaving survivors at the mercy of their fellow humans. The

---

[22]Joseph E. Stiglitz, "Liçoes de Tsunami negra," *O Globo,* year LXXXI, no., 26,347, Sunday, September 25, 2005, 7.

[23]"Depois da tragédia, a barbárie," *Jornal Extra,* Rio da Janeiro, Friday, September 2, 2005, 11.

scenes of vandalism and violence which the people of New Orleans lived through also remind one of the *Ensayo sobre la ceguera* (Essay on Blindness) by the Portuguese author José Saramago, in which an epidemic of blindness thrusts a city into chaos due to the lack of order and official direction. This in turn led to vandalism and unchecked acts of violence which finally ended up in a state of open warfare. In a city with a history of slavery and racial discrimination, the hurricane unmasked these social inequalities and the blindness of the Bush administration.[24]

When we are overwhelmed by natural catastrophes, we tend to think of God. Is God present with us, or absent from us, in these disasters? In times of great natural disasters, many lose what they have, and sometimes even their lives. It is especially the poor who are the most affected. Be it in the Caribbean, in Central America, or in the United States, the poorest and the least protected are the ones who suffer most from earthquakes and hurricanes. People of African descent in the southern states, whose story has been told in American films like *Mississippi Burning,* by Alan Parker, or *The Color Purple*, a reference to the "exotic" and to the "other,"[25] are the victims of Hurricane Katrina, and their culture, found in their music, literature, films and culinary arts, is threatened.[26]

Earthquakes and hurricanes are ways in which nature expressed itself. And Katrina has revealed the insensitivity of the Bush administration. Two hundred seventy-one schools have been closed or damaged and more than 135,000 students in Louisiana, 40,000 students in Mississippi, and 35,000 students in Alabama are without classrooms. The dramatic scenes on the streets and the surrounding area in New Orleans exposed the lack of preparation, the inefficiency and the slow response of

---

[24]Renato Galeano, "Depois da tragédia, a degradaçao da alma humana," *O Globo,* year LXXXI, second edition, Sunday, September 4, 2005, 39.

[25]Jaime Biaggio, "Un lugar mais mítico do que real," *O Globo,* yYear LXXXI, Sunday, September 18, 2005, 39.

[26]Jamari França, "Um fusão única de culturas no berço do jazz," *O Globo*, year LXXXI, second edition, Sunday, September 4, 2005, 38. Antonio Carlos Miguel, "Cultura, a vítima silenciosa do furação," *O Globo*, year LXXXI, Sunday, September 18, 2005, 39.

the Federal Emergency Management Agency, the National Guard, and the Army Corps of Engineers in the United States. The National Guard should have been ready to come to the aid of the people of New Orleans, rather than occupying Iraq. At least a considerable part of the people of the United States would see it this way, knowing that the reconstruction of New Orleans will cost at least one hundred billion dollars, about the same as the United States spends on the Iraq war in six months.[27]

In the context of his protest to the princes who were persecuting the Anabaptists in the sixteenth century, Menno Simons said: "Stand in awe of Him who encloses the heavens and the earth in the palm of His hand, who sends forth the fiery shafts of His lightning, the blasts of the tempests, and makes the mountains to shake, who rules all things with the Word of His power, before whom every knee shall bow of things in heaven and things in earth and things under the earth, and to whom every tongue shall confess that He is the Lord."[28]

When we compare Cecilia Espinoza's vision concerning earthquakes and natural disasters with that of Menno Simons, we find notable similarities. Both refer to the lordship of God over all creation, even when the lightning flashes and tempests roar, causing the mountains to quake. In the second place, both see catastrophes and quakes as a way of relativizing all human claims to power and glory. Third, natural disasters reveal our human fragility in the face of the forces of nature. And finally, in the fourth place, in Cecilia's vision, as well as in Menno's, there is a dynamic relationship between heaven and earth: the Creator's will, in the midst of quakes and hurricanes, is present in the Word.

In the earthly dimension of the vision we note again an emphasis on gentleness and tenderness in caring for one another as the fundamental element that joins it to the heavenly

---

[27]Helena Celestino, "Bush enfrenta o desafío Katrina. Recuperação de Nova Orleans deve custar o mesmo que seis meses de guerra no Iraque," *O Globo*, year LXXXI, second edition, Sunday, September 4, 2005, 37.

[28]John C. Wenger, (Ed.), *The Complete Writings of Menno Simons, c. 1496-1561* (Scottdale, Pa.: Herald Press, 1974), 612-613.

dimension of the vision. While she is above, Cecilia's limbs are restored, and with the Word in her hand she comforts her people, speaking to them words of assurance in times of anxiety and fear. When the love of God is poured out like the sun from the Word it draws Cecilia's attention away from herself, and she hears the cries of the terrified people on the earth. She stands in heaven with her limbs restored, with the Word of God in her hands, and now her voice, like rays from the sun, reaches the earth to comfort her people. Her voice is heard in that great circle of humanity telling them not to fear because God is with them. The upper and lower dimensions of her vision appear to embrace each other by the power of solidarity and comfort.

Out of her personal experience of physical suffering, out of her identification with suffering Job, out of her encounter with Jesus of Nazareth and the God of life, out of a heart filled with tender kindness, Cecilia's actions of compassionate solidarity flow out to those filled with terror and fear in a broken world. Cecilia's vision recalls the prayer which Menno once prayed in solidarity with those who, in his own time, suffered in their broken world: "Do not forsake me, gracious Lord, for trees of deepest root are torn up by the roots by the violence of the storm, and lofty, firm mountains are rent asunder by the force of the earthquake. Did not Job and Jeremiah, dear men of Thy love, stumble in temptation, murmur against Thy will? Suffer me not, therefore, gracious Lord, to be tempted above that I am able to bear, for Thou art faithful and good, lest my soul be shamed. I pray not for my flesh, being well aware that it must suffer and die in time, but this alone I ask: Strengthen me in warfare; assist and keep me; make a way for me to escape in temptation; deliver me, and let me not be put to shame, for I put my trust in Thee."[29]

---

[29]Ibid., 82.

The vision from the earth: The life-giving and comforting Word

What is the mission of the church in the midst of tragedy and human suffering caused by natural disasters? Our word, in the midst of tragedy and suffering caused by earthquakes and hurricanes, must be a message of hope, a caring voice of understanding and kindness. In Cecilia's vision her voice was that of the Word of God. Therefore it was a voice that brought comfort to those suffering from the brokeness of the earth. In the experience of Mennonite communities, our theology and our practice of peace have grown out of the love with which God has taught us to share through compassionate action. In the case of the Caribbean and Central America, the Mennonite Central Committee has served as a living expression of loving kindness that flows out precisely in those times of greatest need among the peoples suffering the effects of natural disasters.

It is important to remember that precisely these disasters have often been the occasions for closely linking North American Mennonites with their sisters and brothers in the Caribbean and in Central America by extending their hands in solidarity and sharing a message of true peace. One of the early expressions of this was the concern of Orie O. Miller, who was then the executive secretary of the Mennonite Central Committee, for the welfare of the Haitian people affected by hurricane Hazel in 1954. It was this sense of solidarity, recorded in his diary in January 1955, that led to the conjoint work of the Mennonite Central Committee and the Missionary Church Association in 1957, and volunteers were sent to Haiti for service in the fields of health and agriculture. Later the island of Haiti would be devastated by Hurricane Flora in October 1963, in which between 1,500 and 4,000 persons would die or disappear. This was followed by Hurricane Inez in September 1966.[30] The Mennonite Central Committee again responded in

---

[30]Following Hurricane Inez, Mennonite Disaster Service (MDS) and Mennonite Central Committee (MCC) worked together in the construction of houses for victims in Cotes de Fer and Marigot. Eldon Stoltzfus, "Haiti," *Mennonite Encyclopedia,* 5:360-361.

compassionate solidarity growing out of a practical understanding of the Word that brings spiritual healing to hearts and puts a roof over the heads of families without shelter.[31]

In Cecilia's vision we noted the gestures of loving kindness that join heaven to earth when she said: "I read the Word and it took on life among all that great multitude of people who were looking up and listening to the stories of *Yan'anjan,* the Creator God and the gentle acts of Jesus in his parables and miracles." In Central America, in the midst of the terrible earthquakes that filled the city of Managua with terror and death in 1972, Guatemala in 1976, and El Salvador in 2001, we can say that we have heard the stories of the Creator God and the gentle acts of loving kindness shown by Mennonite sisters and brothers. In 1998, Hurricane Mitch destroyed Tegucigalpa, Honduras, and a large part of the city of Managua, Nicaragua, leaving in its path of destruction, death and impoverishment throughout Central America. With acts of compassion and loving kindness Mennonite sisters and brothers through their churches and Mennonite Central Committee came to our aid with food, clothing, and shelter for many families who had been left without resources.

This is the true message of a peace that is built, not motivated by self-interests or by those politically based interests in the restoration of a faded image. Rather, it is the power that flows from the parables and the miracles of love. A true theology of peace is interested in doing acts of loving kindness for the healing of broken bodies, with prayer, with the Word, and in concrete expressions of compassionate solidarity. I am certain that the same acts of tender loving care that Cecilia saw in her vision continue to find expression today in the efforts to aid those victims affected by Katrina and Rita. And here I think of the families of African descent, the Hispanics, and the most impoverished families in New Orleans, Louisiana, and Texas.

---

[31]Elaine Stoltzfus, *Tending the Vision, Planting the Seed: A History of the Mennonite Central Committee in Haiti, 1958-1984* (S. l., s. n.), 12-14, 104-107.

Laguna de Guadalupe, Oaxaca, Mexico. (Jaime Prieto Valladares)

get in touch with the world we inhabit, so that our world can also come into communion with us.

The final picture we find painted in Cecilia's vision reminds us of the New Jerusalem, seen by John the Revelator in the shining light of God's sun of righteousness (Rev. 22:1-5). Central to the concept of discipleship in the Anabaptist tradition was life in community. In this vision, we are also faced by the ecclesiological challenge to life in community. Life in this larger community is inclusive and must extend beyond the boundaries of our ecclesial and organizational structures as Mennonites.

The question facing us is how we can get on with the task of reconnecting ourselves to God and God to us. How will we move forward with the task of reconnecting with nature and allowing nature to do the same with us? How can we broaden the missionary task and our ecumenical relationships in such a way that our understanding of the changes that God is bringing to our planet will be an occasion for us to collaborate with other cultural, ecclesial, and organizational traditions, with other spiritual movements, as well as movements within our civic societies, who are concerned about our enslavement to a materialistic view of work, the threats that hang over humanity, the ecological and macro-economical disequilibrium on our planet, and our mindless state of warfare? It is important to catch the vision. But when it comes it will also be important to share it with others, making this vision of God a reality in our midst.

Cecilia's utopian vision ends by summing up the immense joy of those who, as a community, work at caring for the environment God has created. We also see this communal dimension in the Trique people in their daily work and in their corn planting. The vision of the human community under the irradiating sunlight of the Word in an environment in which joy abounds is utopian. Her vision is open to the utopia that binds heaven to earth. From heaven the sun of God's compassionate love and tender kindness shines with the warmth of God's Word. God's life giving message comes to us within God's first book – nature. It also come to us through God's second book – the Word.

Conclusion

Today we seek to recover the vision of our Trique sister, the meaning of co-existence among ourselves and with nature, as well as with our environment. Yan'anjan, the Creator God of Cecilia Espinoza, must come and restore us in a new kind of mission and fill our hearts with the sun of the Word. It is my hope that Cecilia's vision will inspire us, as a community of the followers of Jesus, and that Yan'anjan will fill us with a tender and loving kindness, as gentle as the dew that falls during those star-studded nights that wrap San Isidro de Morelos y La Laguna de Guadalupe.

Index

www.ingramcontent.com/pod-product-compliance
Lightning Source LLC
Chambersburg PA
CBHW051738090426
42738CB00010B/2311